General Editor: Simon Trussler

Associate Editor: Malcolm Page

File on
HARE

Compiled by Malcolm Page

Methuen Drama

A Methuen Drama Book
First published in 1990 as a paperback original
by Methuen Drama, Michelin House,
81 Fulham Road, London SW3 6RB,
and HEB Inc., 70 Court Street, Portsmouth,
New Hampshire 03801, USA

Copyright in the compilation
©1990 by Malcolm Page
Copyright in the series format
©1990 by Methuen Drama
Copyright in the editorial presentation
©1990 by Simon Trussler

Typeset in 9/10 Times by
L. Anderson Typesetting,
Woodchurch, Kent TN26 3TB

Printed in Great Britain
by Cox & Wyman Ltd, Reading

ISBN 0-413-15620-6

British Library Cataloguing in Publication Data
is available from the British Library

Contents

General Editor's Introduction 5

1: A Brief Chronology 7

2: The Plays

a: Original Plays 10
Inside Out 10
How Brophy Made Good 10
What Happened to Blake 10
Slag 11
Deathshead 14
Lay By 14
The Great Exhibition 15
England's Ireland 17
Man above Men 18
Brassneck 19
Knuckle 22
Fanshen 27
Teeth 'n' Smiles 31
Licking Hitler 36
Deeds 39
Plenty 40
Dreams of Leaving 50
A Map of the World 52
Saigon 57
Wetherby 58
Pravda 62
The Bay at Nice 67
Wrecked Eggs 69
The Knife 71
The Secret Rapture 73
Paris by Night 77
Strapless 79

b: Translation 80

3: The Writer on His Work 81

4: A Select Bibliography 84

The theatre is, by its nature, an ephemeral art: yet it is a daunting task to track down the newspaper reviews, or contemporary statements from the writer or his director, which are often all that remain to help us recreate some sense of what a particular production was like. This series is therefore intended to make readily available a selection of the comments that the critics made about the plays of leading modern dramatists at the time of their production — and to trace, too, the course of each writer's own views about his work and his world.

In addition to combining a uniquely convenient source of such elusive *documentation*, the 'Writer-Files' series also assembles the *information* necessary for readers to pursue further their interest in a particular writer or work. Variations in quantity between one writer's output and another's, differences in temperament which make some readier than others to talk about their work, and the variety of critical response, all mean that the presentation and balance of material shifts between one volume and another: but we have tried to arrive at a format for the series which will nevertheless enable users of one volume readily to find their way around any other.

Section 1, 'A Brief Chronology', provides a quick conspective overview of each playwright's life and career. *Section 2* deals with the plays themselves, arranged chronologically in the order of their composition: information on first performances, major revivals, and publication is followed by a brief synopsis (for quick reference set in slightly larger, italic type), then by a representative selection of the critical response, and of the dramatist's own comments on the play and its theme.

Section 3 offers concise guidance to each writer's work in non-dramatic forms, while *Section 4*, 'The Writer on His Work', brings together comments from the playwright himself on more general matters of construction, opinion, and artistic development. Finally, *Section 5* provides a bibliographical guide to other primary and secondary sources of further reading, among which full details will be found of works cited elsewhere under short titles, and of collected editions of the plays — but not of individual titles, particulars of which will be found with the other factual data in Section 2.

The 'Writer-Files' hope by striking this kind of balance between information and a wide range of opinion to offer 'companions' to the study of major playwrights in the modern repertoire — not in that dangerous pre-digested fashion which can too readily quench the desire to read the plays themselves, nor so prescriptively as to allow any single line of approach to predominate, but rather to encourage readers to form their own judgements of the plays in a wide-ranging context.

David Hare began writing in 1968 — the watershed year which identified his generation, and in which, with Howard Brenton and Snoo Wilson, he helped to form Portable Theatre. And it was of an early play for Portable, about William Blake, that Hare remarked, as recorded on page 11, that he didn't find 'artists going bananas' very interesting — 'it's their job to stay sane'. Of all his contemporaries, it is therefore unsurprising that he is the one who most often seems to be writing with a scalpel dipped in ink, cutting incisively yet (or so it seems) dispassionately into the flesh of the British body politic.

As his comments elsewhere in this volume affirm, the condition of Britain — more accurately, of England — is very much Hare's subject. Despite (maybe because of) his own orthodox background, his anatomizing is not usually so much of the political establishment as of those who gather with discreet greed around its lower reaches. And when, in *Knuckle*, he transplanted the idiom of Raymond Chandler into deepest Surrey, his contempt for the raw capitalist ethic remained controlled, even grudgingly admiring: here was a 'morality' which at least displayed ingenuity in its struggle to survive. As Hare later acknowledged, *Knuckle* 'foreshadows the arrival of Mrs. Thatcher'.

When Howard Brenton contributes own inspired bananas to their collaborative works, the results have been at once seamless and explosive. Yet the unexpected popular success of *Pravda* — as of Caryl Churchill's *Serious Money* — revealed its intended victims' delight in collecting the shrapnel which had been meant to wound. Hare's solo work, *The Secret Rapture*, denied audiences that luxury, but puzzled them instead. If, as Hare suggests on page 75, this play is about 'the psychology of Thatcherism' yet is also 'unfashionable . . . in that it is a tragedy', what, beyond resignation, is held in prospect? For 'secret rapture', as Hare points out, is death — which doesn't achieve social change any more than Maggie's burning down of the wine tent in *Teeth'n'Smiles*, or Susan Traherne's foredoomed attempts to recapture the wartime spirit in *Plenty*, all those years and illusions ago.

The filming of *Plenty* affirmed Hare's continuing appeal to a West End style of audience which ought to be at odds with his views. If Shaw became a licensed jester to the classes he attacked, Hare is their house surgeon, telling them the worst with scrupulous bedside manners. The patient, however, so far from dying and making the operation a success, lingers out the last days of capitalism as if tomorrow never came.

Simon Trussler

1947 5 June, born, in St. Leonard's-on-Sea, Sussex: moved to Bexhill at age of five.

1960 Boarder at Lancing. 'I enjoyed it a great deal. . . . It was a liberal, arty public school, then. Very decadent' (*Theatre Quarterly* interview).

1965-68 Read English at Jesus College, Cambridge, taking BA. 'I did direct a couple of shows while I was there. Apart from that, I felt I was wasting my time' (*Theatre Quarterly* interview).

1968 Worked briefly for A. B. Pathé, looking at Pathé Pictorials seeking material for sex education films. Then founded Portable Theatre with Tony Bicât, to tour plays to places without theatres. First play for Portable, *Inside Out*, about Kafka.

1969 Directed *Christie in Love* (Howard Brenton) and *Purity* (D. Mowat) for Portable. Became Literary Manager at Royal Court: the job was 'the sheer grind of reading through umpteen manuscripts. But it financed the work that was important to me, and left me some time as well' (*Theatre Quarterly* interview).

1970 First play, *How Brophy Made Good*, written for Portable. Directed *Christie in Love* and *Fruit* (Brenton) at Theatre Upstairs. *Slag* staged at Hampstead: won *Evening Standard* Award. *What Happened to Blake* performed by Portable. Married Margaret Matheson: two sons, one daughter (divorced, 1980).

1971 One of seven authors on *Lay By*, Portable and Traverse co-production at Edinburgh Festival. Directed *Blow Job* (Snoo Wilson) for Portable. Resigned as Artistic Director of Portable. Translated Pirandello's *Rules of the Game* for a National Theatre production.

1972 *The Great Exhibition* staged at Hampstead. Wrote film script, *Somewhere in England*, from novel by Reg Gadney (unproduced). One of seven authors of *England's Ireland*, and formed Shot, branch of Portable, to tour it.

1973 *Man above Men*, first television play, transmitted,

March. *Brassneck,* co-authored with Howard Brenton, staged at Nottingham, Sept.

1974 *Knuckle*, his first play in London's West End, March. Directed Trevor Griffiths's *The Party* for a National Theatre tour.

1975 Co-founder of Joint Stock: devised *Fanshen* for the company in workshops, toured from March. *Teeth'n'Smiles* performed at Royal Court, Sept.

1976 Directed Howard Brenton's *Weapons of Happiness* at National Theatre.

1977 Awarded US/UK Bicentennial Fellowship, travelling 1977-78, and writing at Daytona Beach, Florida. Directed his own *Licking Hitler*, his first experience of directing for television (transmitted Jan. 1978, and received BAFTA Award).

1978 Co-authored *Deeds*, performed at Nottingham in March. Directed his own *Plenty* at National Theatre in April.

1979 Directed his own *Dreams of Leaving* for television, transmitted Jan. 1980.

1981 Directed *Total Eclipse*, by Christopher Hampton, at Lyric Th., Hammersmith.

1982 Directed the premiere of his *A Map of the World* in Adelaide, and *Plenty* in New York.

1983 Directed *A Map of the World* at the National Theatre. TV play, *Saigon*, transmitted.

1984 Appointed Associate Director of National Theatre.

1985 Wrote and directed his film, *Wetherby* (Golden Bear Award). Directed his *Pravda*, co-authored with Howard Brenton, at the National Theatre, and *A Map of the World* in New York. Film of *Plenty* (scripted by Hare) released. Made a Fellow of the Royal Society of Literature.

1986 Directed his double-bill *The Bay at Nice* and *Wrecked Eggs* at the National Theatre in Sept., and *King Lear*, with Anthony Hopkins in the title-role, there in Dec.

1987 Directed his musical, *The Knife*, in New York.

1988 Wrote and directed two films, *Paris by Night* (released June 1989) and *Strapless*. His *The Secret Rapture* performed at the National Theatre in October. Supported the 'socialist philosophy group' formed by Harold Pinter, Lady Antonia Fraser and others.

1989 Gave Raymond Williams Lecture at Hay-on-Wye Literary Festival in May.

a: Original Plays

All Hare's work, including that for film and television, and collaborations, has been listed consecutively, in order to show the development of his thinking most clearly.

Inside Out

A one-act play, with Tony Bicât.
First production: Arts Lab., Drury Lane, by Portable Th.,
   Sept. 1968.
Unpublished.
Adaptation of Kafka's *Diaries*.

How Brophy Made Good

First production: Brighton Combination, by Portable Th.,
   Mar. 1969; toured to Traverse, Edinburgh, 1 Apr. 1969.
Published: Gambit, No. 17, 1971, p. 84-125 (dir. Hare and
   Tony Bicât).

The making and unmaking of Brophy as short-lived, corrupted TV star. Also about homosexuality versus heterosexuality, and the naivety of revolutionary thinking at the time.

I can say almost nothing about it now. I didn't like it very much when I saw it, and I don't think it's a particularly interesting piece of work.
> Hare, 'From Portable Theatre to Joint Stock',
> *Theatre Quarterly*, Dec. 1975-Feb. 1976, p. 109-10

What Happened to Blake

First production: Theatre Upstairs, in a double bill with

Howard Brenton's *Fruit*, by Portable Th., 28 Sept. 1970, and touring (dir. Tony Bicât).
Unpublished.

Blake was a man I had wanted to write about, and it also meant I could develop a line of work that Portable was doing, a kind of stripping down of stage craft. Though I think *Blake* came out like an imitation of a La Mama play, like a Paul Foster play. I admired Blake, and loved his poems. But I found his madness useless. I don't think artists going bananas are very interesting, it's their job to stay sane. That contradiction in my attitude to him blew the play apart, I couldn't handle it. The most successful passages in the play are about Mrs. Blake, for whom I have a great deal of time.

> Hare, 'From Portable Theatre to Joint Stock',
> *Theatre Quarterly*, No. 20, Dec. 1975-Feb. 1976, p. 110

Delving into costumes scattered round the stage, the cast of five offer us a capsule account of William Blake's career, rightly stress that to him the external world was one continued vision of fancy and imagination and (more questionably) portray eighteenth-century literary society as trivial, self-admiring, and inbred. What worries me is that the jokey strip-cartoon style (Jane Austen enters on roller-skates singing 'Falling in Love Again,' two khaki-clad actors brandishing panto-prop swords send up Blake's heroic drama) tends to diminish Blake himself and leave us with the impression that he was simply a revolutionary loony who was unbelievably callous in his personal relationships.

> Michael Billington, 'Portable Theatre',
> *Plays and Players*, Nov. 1970, p. 49

Slag

A play in two acts.
First production: Hampstead Th. Club, 6 Apr. 1970
(dir. Roger Hendricks Simon; with Rosemary McHale as Joanne, Marty Cruickshank as Elise, and Diane Fletcher as Ann).
Revived: Royal Court, 24 May 1971 (dir. Max Stafford-Clark, with Lynn Redgrave as Joanne, Barbara Ferris as Elise, and Anna Massey as Ann).
First U.S. production: Other Stage, Public Th., New York, 21 Feb. 1971

(dir. Roger Hendricks Simon).
Published: Faber, 1971; *Plays and Players*, June 1970, p. 61-77.

---

*Three women teachers at Brackenhurst, a girls' boarding school
(who are in imminent danger of outnumbering their pupils),
have entered into a treaty to abstain from sex, and so uphold the
glory of womanhood and the superiority of the clitoris. Joanne
is a would-be revolutionary and film-addict; Elise is a neurotic
who almost achieves pregnancy by an act of the imagination;
and Ann, the eldest, the headmistress, is full of old school ties
and sporting inclinations, the local butcher among them. Scenes
of visual ingenuity — episodes in a shower and at a cricket
match — are interspersed with quarrels between the women,
who are finally deserted by the last pupil. At the end, they hover
between cutting the sado-masochistic cord that binds them and
starting again from scratch next term.*

I regarded *Slag* as an exercise for the proscenium arch — using what I
had learned with Portable. It was meant to conjure up everything out of
the air — the empty space which is almost always the starting point for a
Portable show.

> Hare, interviewed by Peter Ansorge, 'Portable Playwrights',
> *Plays and Players*, Feb. 1972, p. 18

The point is that it's really a play about institutions, not about women at
all. Only that I thought it was delightful to see three women on the stage.
It's about every institution I had known — school, Cambridge, Pathé,
and so on. They are all the same. That is how institutions perpetuate
themselves. With rituals that go on inside them — ever more baroque
discussions about ever dwindling subjects. But it happens to be peopled
with women, partly because it was the sort of play that I thought I would
enjoy going to see — women on the stage, represented as I thought more
roundly and comprehensively than was then usual.

> Hare, 'From Portable Theatre to Joint Stock',
> *Theatre Quarterly*, Dec. 1975-Feb. 1976, p. 110-11

The second half of the play peters out in a string of fantastications
involving a phantom pregnancy — which despite a lively flow of jokes,
must be said to sum up the whole idea, or jape. Mr. Hare leaves us in no

doubt that he regards women as pretty silly, helpless creatures if left to their own devices.

J. W. Lambert, 'Plays in Performance', *Drama*, Autumn 1971, p. 20

Where the original production at the Hampstead Theatre Club tried with gentleness as well as wild humour to explore the relationships of three women bound to each other by a view of society, the Royal Court has gone all out for the easy laughs. . . . The recipe — part old, part new, part borrowed, part blue — could hardly fail. You start with a girls' school and the more obvious shades of St. Trinians and onto this graft the hilarious — from a man's point of view — theme of women trying to go it on their own. You trick it out with the trendiest intellectual targets of the 'seventies — women's lib, revolutionary cant, the sending up of true romance, a little dubious sex play, sufficient to alarm the *Sunday Times*. . . . I disapprove of it. It's cheap, easy, exaggerated caricature. I laughed a lot and every time I did so I felt a traitor to my sex.

Mary Holland, *Plays and Players*, July 1971, p. 32, 56

It's an extremely funny play, with touches of brilliance. . . . The plot of *Slag* is a cross between *Princess Ida* and Evelyn Waugh's *Decline and Fall*. Three young women set up a girl's boarding-school which they resolve will be an experiment in all-female living. In no time, their nursling comes apart in a series of disasters which make Waugh's Llanaba Abbey seem by comparison as gleaming a model of educational efficiency as Harvard Business School. Children leave in droves. Mistresses try to tunnel their way to freedom. The head and her assistant turn to lesbianism, resulting in a phantom pregnancy. But in the Hampstead production, there was another dimension. The three girls inhabited a masculine fantasy, and knew it. 'This can't be happening', cried one, 'women don't behave like this'. Fleeing from a world where male dominance trapped them in 'womanly' roles, they found themselves equally trapped by their attempt to live opposite ones. Whatever they did, they moved under the controlling, derisive eyes of man. Largely, this was the result of Rosemary McHale's performance as the most militantly feminist of the trio. Paranoiac, sly, and self-doubting, armoured in women's lib texts and the jargon of cinema magazines, she was at once funny and tragic, passionate and self-caricaturing. It was a remarkable display, making the play sharply comic, in a way unlike any other you'd ever seen.

Ronald Bryden, 'All Girls Together in Chelsea',
The Observer, 30 May 1971

Slag is unfocused and sometimes boring, but it is attractively articulate and theatrically at home. . . . The best aspect of the play is that Hare has taken a conventional comedy about a public-school staff and converted it *internally* into a macabre fantasy without much altering externals, rather in the manner of I. Compton-Burnett. Some of the materials are: a kind of mod *Princess Ida*, a female sanctum with males excluded and the results thereof; satire on cultural glibness; and, the seeming *sine qua non* of English playwrights these days, a microcosm of the fate of the Empire. None of these efforts wholly succeeds, largely because Hare never clarifies his viewpoint, he just has fun.

Stanley Kauffmann, *New Republic*, 13 Mar. 1971, p. 32

See also:

Ruby Cohn, 'Shakespeare Left', *Theatre Journal*, March 1988, p. 48-60. [Influence of *Love's Labour's Lost*; also about Edward Bond, Howard Brenton, David Edgar, and Arnold Wesker.]

Deathshead

A very short play.
First production: Traverse Th., Edinburgh, December 1971.
Unpublished.

That one lasts two minutes. It was written for the Traverse, for a Christmas show. It's about a disastrous Christmas party at which someone contracts VD — it's about the intensity of people's experiences in VD clinics. The only reason it's at Christmas is that the Traverse wanted a Christmas play. I think there were eight writers altogether, or maybe ten, who contributed to this show, and we all disgraced ourselves, except Stanley Eveling.

Hare, 'From Portable Theatre to Joint Stock', *Theatre Quarterly*, Dec. 1975-Feb. 1976, p. 111

Lay By

A two-act play, written with Howard Brenton, Brian Clark, Trevor

Griffiths, Steven Poliakoff, Hugh Stoddart, and Snoo Wilson.
First production: Portable Th. and Traverse co-production,
   Traverse Th., Edinburgh, 24 Aug. 1971 (dir. Snoo Wilson).
First London production: Th. Upstairs, 26 Sept. 1971.
Published: Calder and Boyars, 1972; *Plays and Players*, Nov. 1971,
   p. 65-75.

Elaboration of a rape case involving a man and two women in a van in a lay by on the M4 motorway.

I'd wanted to write a script with a lot of other people. And so we said to everyone at the meeting [at the Royal Court]: 'would those of you who'd like to write a script together please put your hands up.' And people like Ken Campbell, Jeff Nuttall, and so on did just that. So we said: 'Would those of you who'd like to partake go to the bar.' And at the bar there were slightly fewer. So we said: 'Those who are interested meet next Wednesday. And then there were fewer and fewer. Most of us didn't know each other, you see. The idea came originally from a newspaper clip about fellatio on a lay-by on the day we first met [Ludovic Kennedy, 'The Case of Colman Lydon', *Sunday Times*, 28 March 1971, p. 32]. . . . It's not something that is generally available to theatre writers, that sort of situation, because it's so much a newspaper story. . . . The thing is that it was very innocent theatrically in the sense that originally it wasn't theatrical thinking, and that's why it's shaped the way it is — a sort of cancerous growth that just grew and grew and grew. It wasn't consciously a question of: 'How do we make a play out of this?' . . . It only grew organically from the content, it never grew from the form. . . . It's a wonderful new liberating way of writing.
   Hare, interviewed by John Ford, 'Getting the Carp out of the Mud',
   Plays and Players, Nov. 1971, p. 20, 83

The play has a unifying style, a combination of verbal surrealism and documentary reportage. . . . Its sustained view of exploitation and its courage in treating sex as indefatigably comic makes *Lay By* a major theatrical event of this or any festival.
   Nicholas de Jongh, *The Guardian*, 26 Aug. 1971

The Great Exhibition

A play in two acts.

The Great Exhibition

First production: Hampstead Th., 28 Feb. 1972 (dir. Richard Eyre; with
   David Warner as Hammett and Penelope Wilton as Maud).
Published: Faber, 1972; *Plays and Players*, May 1972, p. 63-81.

*The hero, Hammett, is a Labour MP. He has chosen to pursue
socialism because he has a talent for it, because he needed some
enthusiasms to get him to the grave (the others are sex and
food), because boredom spreads about him like contagion.
Unfortunately all this does not make him into a socialist. His
politics fall short of action. There was a time when he pursued
at least a parliamentary road with some energy, but now he
has withdrawn completely even from that. He does not go to the
House of Commons and has given up the visits to his northern
constituency ('Well, it's a long way and when you get there it's
a dump'). Now he, sits around his colour-supplement flat
(William Morris prints and pot growing under the spotlight)
contemplating his sense of isolation, setting a private detective
on his wife, and worrying away at his sense of emptiness like
an old scab. When his wife leaves him he makes a last foray into
action, to do something impossible by exposing himself on
Clapham Common. In the event most of his victims are unim-
pressed, and the one person who takes some notice turns out to
be his wife's best friend. Maud, his wife, is as isolated as
Hammett himself. She works in the theatre — 'the most
sophisticated possible means of ignoring what people are
actually like' — but married him in the hope that through him
she would make contact with real life. Now that he seems to
have withdrawn into neurotic self-absorption, she tries to
establish that contact for herself, first by taking a lover then
by taking over his constituency. Both efforts are doomed to
failure.*

Mary Holland, *Plays and Players*, Apr. 1972, p. 40

The 'seriousness' of many plays is just another word for self-pity. To me
a cultivated seriousness is only so much phoney suffering. *The Great
Exhibition* is about people who suffer with a capital S — that area of
self-ignorance.

Hare, interviewed by Peter Ansorge, 'Portable Playwrights',
Plays and Players, Feb. 1972, p. 18

Mr. Hare's play seems to be built on a rancorous dislike of the generation that preceded him. . . . I'll say this for Mr. Hare: he certainly lets you know what he dislikes. The encyclopaedic list includes parliamentary democracy, privileged middle-class despair, unfeeling upper-class arrogance, fake hippiedom, verbal culture, Ibsenite drama, avant-garde posturing, and George Orwell. But the problem is that a play has to be founded on something more than a rejection of all that has gone before unless it is to dwindle into peevishness; and although there is a case to be made against, say, the British parliamentary system or radical protest, it needs to be specific and accurate and not a blanket condemnation full of off-the-peg cynicism. What saves the play is Mr. Hare's bilious wit (I like the idea of someone dying of 'terminal acne') and his spry sense of farce (a lugubrious private eye is constantly popping unexpectedly out of cupboards).

Michael Billington, *The Guardian*, 1 Mar. 1972

England's Ireland

A documentary play in two acts, with Tony Bicât, Howard Brenton, Brian Clark, David Edgar, Francis Fuchs, and Snoo Wilson.
First production: by Shoot at Mickery Th., Amsterdam, Sept. 1972.
First London production: Royal Court, 2 Oct. 1972, and Round House, 9 Oct., both for one night; and touring to Glasgow, Lancaster and Nottingham.
Unpublished.

Includes a brief history of British political involvement in Northern Ireland since 1920; a statement of the loyalist viewpoint; the civil rights march of 1969, led by Bernadette Devlin; a TV interview of 1992 with an elderly British colonel, looking back on the army's role; and a dramatization of British military regulations about firing on civilians. The second half includes an Irish comic telling racist Irish jokes; a Protestant Masonic ceremony followed by a UDA military exercise; a priest hearing a Catholic woman's last confession; and Provo and Official IRA members discussing their views.

It was written much more intensely than *Lay By*, with the writers going away and staying in the country together. But then when Snoo Wilson and I came to sit down and analyze it we found we didn't have a play: so that last third was written by just Snoo and me — not the last third chronologically, that is, but the chewing-gum third.

> Hare, 'From Portable Theatre to Joint Stock', *Theatre Quarterly*,
> Dec. 1975-Feb. 1976, p. 113

If you're involved in a collaborative work like *England's Ireland*, you stop short at the minimal agreeable statements. You stop short at the lowest common denominator which in this case seemed to be along the lines that the fighting in Northern Ireland was blatantly a result of a colonial situation, that the English stance of neutral intervention was a farce, and that the army should withdraw as quickly as possible while a minimal political programme for the country was devised. That may seem despicably little to say about the situation but at the time those things were barely being said in public at all. . . . We just flogged ourselves to death on a show . . . which it then proved impossible to bring to public attention. The English theatre as a whole, and with more resolution than I've ever seen them muster, got together and said no in thundering tones to the idea of a show about a British civil war. We were totally exhausted by this reaction. It was very traumatic.

> Hare, interviewed by Peter Ansorge, 'Current Concerns',
> *Plays and Players*, July 1974, p. 19

Their human sympathies are with the native Irish proletariat, oppressed, as they see it, by the ascendancy of implacable colonists, by an inequitable economic system, and by their own Church; and their political sympathies are accordingly nearer Sinn Fein than any other faction. They don't take this position straightforwardly or without reservations. . . . Inevitably, there are omissions, concrete and philosophical: too little historical background. . . . A vast amount of disparate matter — statistics, ideas, satire, song, theatrical dialogue — has been subsumed into something which the sustained concern of the writing and the disciplined energy of a good cast renders pretty coherent in feeling and tone.

> Benedict Nightingale, 'Fair Partisans',
> *New Statesman*, 6 Oct. 1972

Man above Men

A television play.

Transmitted: 'Play for Today', BBC, 19 Mar. 1973 (dir. Alan Clarke;
    with Gwen Watford as Susan and Alexander Knox as the Judge).
Unpublished.

It wrote itself, I just sat down and wrote it, which I've never done before
or since. It was a play about a judge and his daughter, who felt that out
of snobbishness she has persecuted her husband, who was dead, because
he was of a different class. And it was also about a series of cases that
were going on in the court where the judge was sitting. I'd been going to
the Old Bailey, and I wanted to write a play about the mind of a judge.
In the end the woman commits suicide, and the play covers the last two
or three days of her life.

> Hare, 'From Portable Theatre to Joint Stock', *Theatre Quarterly*,
> Dec. 1975-Feb. 1976, p. 115

I found this piece glibber than a barker's spiel. A two-part contention
between an ailing judge and his questioning daughter, it took place in a
loopy ambience that rang bells all over the memory-circuit: the author, I
think, has been boning up on his 'forties Broadway. The play was slickly
built, but the characters kept sliding out of character.

> Clive James, *The Observer*, 25 Mar. 1973

Brassneck

A play in three acts, with Howard Brenton.
First production: Nottingham Playhouse, 19 Sept. 1973 (dir. Hare; with
    Paul Dawkins as Alfred Bagley and Myles Hoyle as Clive Avon).
Television production: 'Play for Today', BBC1, 22 May 1975 (dir. Mike
    Newell; with Jeremy Kemp as Roderick Bagley and Andrew Ray as
    Clive Avon).
Published: Eyre Methuen, 1974; *Plays and Players*, Oct. 1973.

*An old man, Alfred Bagley, comes to a small town in the
Midlands in 1945 and sets up a property business with £50. He
rises to the position of Master of the local Masonic Lodge, and
brings his nephew Roderick into his business. After Alfred's
death at his grand-niece's wedding, Roderick, his poet wife, and
their two sons expand the business into Europe, Asia, and*

Africa. The local politicians eat out of their hands until they run into bankruptcy and charges of bribery. Finally there is a reunion at the behest of Sidney, Roderick's son, at his strip club, 'The Lower Depths', in the 1970s. Sidney persuades the family of the profits of importing heroin, and the play ends with a toast to 'the last days of capitalism'.

Reading Angus Calder's *The People's War* changed all my thinking as a writer; an account of the Second World War through the eyes of ordinary people, it attempts a complete alternative history to the phoney and corrupting history I was taught at school. Howard Brenton and I attempted in *Brassneck* to write what I have no doubt Calder would still write far better than we, an imagined subsequent volume, *The People's Peace*, as seen, in our case, through the lives of the petty bourgeoisie, builders, solicitors, brewers, politicians, the masonic gang who carve up provincial England. It was my first step into the past.

> Hare, 'A Lecture given at King's College, Cambridge',
> *Licking Hitler*, p. 66

Brassneck was a clear instance of a play which did catch on with a far wider audience than normally went to the theatre. . . . It worked on the lowest common denominator. Howard and I stopped short at exactly the point where we began to diverge politically in our approach to the subject. *Brassneck* is as far as Howard and I can go in agreement. The play ends with the simple statement that these are 'the last days of capitalism'. On how exactly the system will be transformed, how the future would shape, we couldn't agree. . . . There is a sense of voracious enjoyment among capitalists themselves that these are their last days and that they're going to go down with all guns blaring.

> Hare, interviewed by Peter Ansorge, 'Current Concerns',
> *Plays and Players*, July 1974, p. 19-20

It worked by opposition of methods. Howard Brenton has a great minestrone of a mind. You plunge the ladle in every morning and it comes out brimming with ideas. Whereas I have difficulty in getting every single idea right.

> Hare, interviewed by Hugh Hebert, 'Putting the Knuckle In',
> *The Guardian*, 4 Mar. 1974

We wanted a show about corruption in England, in a town like

Nottingham, but neither of us felt that independently we were wise enough to write it, so we decided to write it together. . . . I feel it's wholly my play, David feels it's wholly his, and yet it's neither of ours. Yet it was. Both of us take full responsibility for it as a work.

Brenton, 'Petrol Bombs through the Proscenium Arch',
Theatre Quarterly, March-May 1975, p. 19

'Brassneck' is a Midlands word meaning 'cheek' or 'nerve'. It has criminal connotations.

'Authors' Note', *Brassneck*, p. 7

London is too complex a society for any play to dissect, but periodically writers like John Arden and David Turner have tried to perform this operation on provincial cities. Howard Brenton and David Hare's *Brassneck* is a pungent and ambitious contribution to this genre. And whatever theatrical risks it takes are entirely a by-product of having something urgent to say. In form it might even sound old-fashioned, being a three-generation family saga with all the attendant Galsworthian ramifications. What most ties the piece to our own time is its sense of social vertigo. For reasons due partly to the characters and partly to outer forces, the rules keep changing and finally what the authors produce is not so much a 25-year family chronicle as a requiem for the age of free enterprise. . . . Their play is not the result of a strong local attachment but of a guerilla raid from which they have picked up enough intelligence to create their all-purpose Midlands town. . . .

If Alfred had not been so cunning, if Roderick had not been such a fool, then the story would have taken a different turning: so in what sense is it true of British society at large? . . . Theatrically the piece is miscalculated in the sense that no other character comes near to rivalling old Alfred, who dies in mid-speech during his wild daughter's Lucullan wedding celebrations. . . . The production covers scenes of golf links, the hunting field, and council offices, not to mention a lurid Vatican fantasy in which Alfred imagines himself crowned Pope. All this is presented with deft perspective, screen projections, and a few solid props.

Irving Wardle, *The Times*, 21 Sept. 1973

Its extraordinary quality is its sense of the accurst. There is an impalpable evil in the wedding scene, and also in the impossible and irresistible picnic, which is outside and independent of the characters themselves. . . . Maeterlinck speaks somewhere of a third person being present in every dialogue in his theatre, enigmatic and invisible, the unconscious but powerful idea that the dramatist has of the universe, who gives to his plays their resonance and reverberations. That person, not named, not embodied, and of course not mentioned in the programme, is what makes *Brassneck* so difficult properly to seize and so impossible to escape from.

Harold Hobson, 'Bold as Brass',
Sunday Times, 23 Sept. 1973

What I like about the play is the way it interweaves family, civic, and national issues. . . . What lifts the play above agitprop is that it indicts left as well as right. Labour councillors and MPs are shown to be as susceptible as anyone else to the creeping magnetism of power; and, though credit is paid to the Attlee government, we are reminded that had they carried out their promise to nationalize land the whole history of post-war Britain would have been different. Moreover, at their best, Brenton and Hare capture something of the strange texture of English provincial life: Masonic initiation rites are presented in all their black-comedy detail, and there's a brilliantly bleary wedding feast, evoking the smell of stale champagne and ending with Bagley senior's nightmare recollection of cannibalism in the First World War trenches. In the end Brenton and Hare waste a lot of their buckshot. Why bother with expense account fiddlers and genteel housewife-poets when there are bigger targets to aim at? And by staking so much on the Bagleys they never really discuss the failures of the system they represent.

Michael Billington, *The Guardian*, 21 Sept. 1973

Knuckle

A play in two acts.
First production: Oxford Playhouse, 29 Jan. 1974
(dir. Michael Blakemore; with Edward Fox as Curly and
Kate Nelligan as Jenny).
First London production: Comedy Th., 4 Mar. 1974.
First New York production: Phoenix Sideshow, Playhouse II,
23 Jan. 1975 (dir. Daniel Freudenberger).
Revived: Hudson Guild, New York, 4 Mar. 1981
(dir. Geoffrey Sherman).
Television productions: PBS, June 1975 (heavily Americanized:
Guildford becomes Los Angeles, Eastbourne Santa Monica, and
London Chicago); BBC2, 7 May 1989 (dir. Moira Armstrong;

with Tim Roth as Curly and Emma Thompson as Jenny).
Published: Faber, 1974; in *The History Plays*, 1984.

Curly, the cynical protagonist of Knuckle, *might seem typecast to step straight into the opening shot or page of any regulation enigmatic thriller: and so, in a way, he is, but there is also quite another side to his profile. A gun seller (not* runner, *he differentiates), he plays down the exotic connotations of the role, insistent he is just as likely to flog his wares in Acton as Peru; and he opted for the job in protest against the prosperously respectable stockbroking belt into which he was born. The return of this native to the Guildford of his boyhood is motivated by his determination to solve the mystery of the disappearance and possible murder of his sister, who has also been a rebel against the complacent family life. But, just as Curly is scarcely the usual adventurer of thick-ear fiction, so the father he challengingly confronts is not quite your typical stockbroker, being a reader not only of Henry James but of music scores too; a polished sinister phoney in headlong class conflict with his polished roughneck son. Within a framework of sets including the `Crumbles at Eastbourne as well as a sleazy Guildford nightclub (imagination boggles!) and the City father's country home, Curly stubbornly interrogates all who knew the vanished girl, throwing insults and accusations all around the smug locale, while persistently equating the small central mystery with the peripheral iniquities of the profit motive.*

Romilly Cavan, 'Scripts', *Plays and Players*, Oct. 1974, p. 48

Knuckle is about what morality is and whether it is any use to us in the last quarter of the century. . . . *Knuckle* is an almost obscenely constructive play! It says something about it being impossible to live within the system without doing yourself moral damage. That's a huge claim. . . . It's a play about knowing, about the fact that there are no excuses, and the fact that people who are damaged by the system know themselves to have been damaged, and are not ignorant of what they've done to themselves. And that is a large claim, because how you feel about capitalists — whether you believe them to be knaves or fools — determines everything you believe and think politically. . . . I particularly wanted to write a play which was accessible to everybody — it's about people for whom political rhetoric is no part of their lives.

The characters aren't political — or intellectual — at all. . . . The reason I don't find the play pessimistic is because it also contains the most admirable person I've ever drawn, this girl who is meant to be a good person. The whole play deals with moral values, and concludes that there *is* such a thing as moral value. That seems to me quite cheerful.

> Hare, 'From Portable Theatre to Joint Stock',
> *Theatre Quarterly*, Dec. 1975-Feb. 1976, p. 113-14

I have no snobbery about thrillers. From childhood they have been the form of literature I have understood best, and my enthusiasm is indiscriminate. . . . If I have a preference at all, it is for those who work against the form to make it do something to which it is not apparently suited. In Patricia Highsmith's books there is no obvious mystery except the mystery of why we are alive. She works against the expectations of the genre to make violent action seem neither colourful nor dramatic but commonplace. . . .

I intended *Knuckle* in fact as an exhibition of capitalism's strengths and some guide to its intense emotional appeal. Capitalism adapts; and in the early 'seventies was adapting faster than usual to a change of mood in England. Underlying *Knuckle* is the feeling that there will no longer be any need for public life to be decked out in morality. In the last days of the Empire, English capitalism still dressed in a bespoke philosophy of service and intended civilization. But now politicians were ready to stand on a platform of bad-tempered self-interest, with only the most formal claims on the electorate's higher feelings. Out for Number One was suddenly to be the acceptable political creed of the day. In this, *Knuckle*, God help us, foreshadows the arrival of Mrs. Thatcher.

> Hare, 'Introduction', *The History Plays*, p. 10

Blakemore's production triumphantly captures the right flavour and idiom, playing the central private-eye situation absolutely straight, letting the satirical and other undertones speak for themselves, and resisting any temptations to overt spoof and satire. If I say that its tone and style reminded me at times of Howard Hawks's film of Chandler's *The Big Sleep* and Jack Smight's more recent movie version of Ross Macdonald's *The Moving Target*, then I cannot pay it a higher tribute than that. His ironic use of a theme tune — Ivor Novello's 'We'll Gather Lilacs in the Spring Again', the archetypal Home Counties melody — is particularly brilliant.

> Jonathan Hammond, *Plays and Players*, Apr. 1974, p. 40

The play's framework is that of a detective novel; the text refers to Mickey Spillane, but the ambience is more that of Raymond Chandler, a classic source for Hollywood right down to *The Long Goodbye*. . . . The writing is marked by wit, intelligence, and a deepening sense of strain; the author becomes the captive of his own idea. Hollywood into Guildford is a good joke, but an imperfect equation, so when Mr. Hare finally starts laying into the Home Counties capitalist ethic it is difficult to take him seriously; like his hero, he is not quite as tough as perhaps he would like to think. And the format presents insoluble narrative problems: in the book you would read the plot passages twice, in the film you would settle for incomprehension and get high on speed and action, but the stage allows neither alternative.

Robert Cushman, *The Observer*, 10 Mar. 1974

In one sense, Curly has come back to unmask the British capitalist swindle. But in another, he is still a little boy aching for a decisive battle with a dominant father. Mr. Hare clearly intends the play to be taken in both ways. But the two largely cancel each other out. Either Curly's puritanism, his appalled reaction to his homeland, and his quest are to be taken seriously; or the whole action becomes an adolescent initiation fantasy. Often it seems to be just that. There is one ludicrous scene where Curly establishes his arms dealing credentials by putting a big order through and discharging a revolver into the audience.

Irving Wardle, 'Revenge Mission in Darkest Guildford',
The Times, 5 Mar. 1974

I must confess at times I was reminded of the over-zealous revolutionary in Shaw's *Misalliance* who cries 'Rome fell, Babylon fell, Hindhead's turn will come'. Moreover, the inherent melodrama of the pulp-thriller seriously undermines the attack on the genuine evils of property speculation. But the play is much subtler than it at first appears. For a start Mr. Hare creates genuine moral uncertainty by making the exposer of corruption himself a lethal barbarian: there is little, in fact, to chose between the gun-toting hero and his city slicker of a father. In reality the work is built round a sustained, intelligent contrast between the volubility of open protest and the discretion, elegance, and quietness of much British capitalism; and in that way it more seriously questions our allegedly 'civilized' values. Moreover, having chosen his style ('That's a very nice leg' — 'I got another one just like it') Mr. Hare also pursues it with total consistency.

Michael Billington, *The Guardian*, 5 Mar. 1974

Curly is, in effect, a Humphrey Bogart hero at least thirty years too late and, failing to win the girl or solve the mystery or stop the villains, he retreats into the black-and-white security of his mini-munitions business. There are some problems with the play — a certain windiness, Hare's not recognizing that the play ends one scene before it stops — but it is the production that is really at fault. Edward Fox's Curly has neither a contemporary reality nor a Bogartian echo; he is a thing of abrupt mannerisms and oddly inflected lines, and he is, unhappily, on stage most of the time.

> Gerald Weales, 'Theatre Journal, London, 1974',
> *North American Review*, Fall 1974

[*Knuckle*] is palpably flawed, yet it clutches your interest, uses language buoyantly, and gives emotional tension a steadily visible dramatic shape. Best of all, it bespeaks unflagging intelligence even where intentions are incompletely realized. . . . By splashing Raymond Chandler with absurdism and letting a convoluted plot drown amid defiantly over-simplified characterizations, Hare tries for a sort of dislocation, further distorted by grandiloquently eccentric but witty verbiage, that would send up the nastiness of suburban London and, by implication, all the complacent, frayed-edged, chipping suburbia of the western world. But the exigencies of genre, and even of caricaturing that genre, prevent the anticapitalist indignation from achieving due substance; despite prodigious verbal flights, fireworks refuse to turn into firebombing, lampooning crumples before the task of lambasting. . . . *Knuckle* is like a piano piece for black keys only: tricky, but not unmusical.

> John Simon, *New York*, 30 Mar. 1981

Even the best political plays of the new generation of playwrights (David Hare's *Knuckle*, Howard Brenton's *Magnificence*) dissipate their own power by presenting the opposition entertainingly enough but neither very accurately nor quite fairly.

> 'Open Stage', *Times Literary Supplement*,
> 24 May 1974, p. 556

The new generation of playwrights . . . may seem less ambitious than their predecessors, but they are also refreshingly more relaxed. Their plays are mostly either directly political like Trevor Griffiths's *Occupations* (1970) and *The Party* (1973) and Howard Brenton's *Magnificence* (1973) and *The Churchill Play* (1974) or political by implication, satirizing the corruption of contemporary capitalist society as in David Hare's *Knuckle* (1974), Brenton and Hare's *Brassneck* (1973), and Snoo Wilson's *The Pleasure Principle* (1973).

John Spurling, 'Freedoms of the City',
Encounter, XLIV, Jan. 1975, p. 66

See also:

Gareth and Barbara Lloyd Evans, eds., *Plays in Review, 1956-1980* (Batsford, 1985), p. 197-8.

William J. Free, 'Mischief and Frustration in David Hare's *Knuckle*', in *The Legacy of Thespis*, ed. Karelisa V. Hartigan (London: University Press of America, 1984), p. 23-9.

Fanshen

A play in two acts, based on the book of the same name by
William Hinton.

First production: by Joint Stock, Crucible Studio, Sheffield,
10 Mar. 1975, and touring (dir. William Gaskill and
Max Stafford-Clark).

First London production: Institute of Contemporary Arts, 21 Apr 1975,
then continued touring, returning to Hampstead Th., London,
12 Aug., then touring to Kirkaldy, Glasgow, Edinburgh, Cardiff,
Winchester, Aldershot, Milton Keynes, and Bletchley.

Television production: BBC2, 18 Oct. 1975.

First American production: Milwaukee Repertory Th., Wisconsin,
Spring 1976.

Published: Faber, 1976; in *The Asian Plays*, 1986; *Plays and Players*,
Sept. 1975, p. 41-50; Oct. 1985, p. 43-50.

The play chronicles the 'education' of the peasants of the Chinese village of Long Bow during the revolution, from 1945 to 1949. For generations the peasants served the land-lords, whose power was unquestioned. They are now forced to question who needs whom, who depends on whom, for what and why. The play charts the process of change in the life of a small community, highlighting their bitter struggle to rationalize old habits and traditions in order to evolve new values, a new order, and the building of a more humane life.

Fanshen is a book of about five or six hundred pages by William Hinton, who was himself in China at the time of the story he describes. He spent some six or eight years writing what he wanted to be the definitive record of one village's life during those years of change. In summer 1974 Bill Gaskill and Max Stafford-Clark asked me to read it and to dramatize it for Joint Stock. . . .

We originally did five weeks' workshop on the six hundred pages, trying all sorts of different approaches to this apparently intractable material. Just in sheer stage-time the book was enormous, but also the problems of presentation seemed to us insuperable. So we tried various kinds of slogan theatre, various ways of telescoping the material, various arts of story-telling, various exercises to do with how to tell the essence of a story in the shortest possible time. . . . The way the play emerged was finally fixed first of all by the two directors and me deciding a scenario and then by me deciding which of the many plays inside Hinton's book I was going to write. And the play *Fanshen* is very different from the book *Fanshen*; both its aims and the play's selection from the book, its route through the book, make it a very different kind of project. It was a personal response to certain themes inside the book, notably the questions how does any democracy know it's a good democracy, how do the led look after the leadership, how do the ruled rule the rulers? It was out of a personal interest in these questions that the play was written. The material in the book that is apparently dramatic I found to be the least dramatic of all; that's to say all the stuff to do with the violence of the early years of the revolution — the first 150 pages of the book, the hangings, shootings, scalps coming away from skulls, trials, uprisings — are, oddly, the undramatic material. . . .

Once the text was written it stood more or less. We changed a few sections — those that always gave difficulty were the scenes of village life where it was necessary to return to some kind of reality in the lives of the peasants, which we found much more difficult than the scenes of argument and debate, which fell out almost at once, almost played themselves. The scenes where we westerners represent the daily life of the village we found much more difficult. Once the play opened and William Hinton — who assumed that the play would fail, as previous attempts to dramatize the book had — heard that it was doing well, he arrived on a plane from America with a whole series of emendations. The play was therefore rethought over and over again between him and the company and between him and me. The finally agreed text is a compromise between him and us simply because the view he takes of the Chinese

Revolution and of events in that village is inevitably a slightly rosier one than that which I and the company took.

> Hare, 'After *Fanshen*: a Discussion', in
> *Performance and Politics in Popular Drama*,
> ed. David Bradby, Louis James, and Bernard Sharratt
> (Cambridge University Press, 1980), p. 297-9

[Hare has also written about the play in the Preface to *Fanshen*, in the Introduction to *The Asian Plays*, and in *The Joint Stock Book*, ed. Rob Ritchie (Methuen, 1987), p. 105-10, which is reprinted from *Granta*, May 1986. Max Stafford-Clark and the actresses Carole Hayman and Pauline Melville also write of the play in *The Joint Stock Book*, p. 110-18.]

The nearest any English contemporary writer has come to emulating Brecht.

> Michael Coveney, 'Green Room',
> *Plays and Players*, Oct. 1975, p. 10

The play is a human rather than a political document. No one is asked to feel elation at the arrival of the Communists or the display of the slogans on their blood-red banners. One is asked only to understand what the imposition of new, strange standards on people accustomed to centuries of tradition can do to them. The simple, low-coloured performance, with little in it in the way of theatrical excitement, shows us the picture without chiaroscuro. I found it extremely interesting; but moving, no.

> B. A. Young, *The Mirror up to Nature*
> (William Kimber, 1982), p. 97

Why wasn't it boring? All those drably quilted peasants with meaning-less names indulging in public self-criticism threaten to be theatrical death. Perhaps it is because the play simply acts out what happened, letting the story tell itself. It is stripped almost bare of individual charac-terization, except in occasional moments of recrimination or frustrated idealism, and this Maoist, if not Confucian, economy of style gives the production an effective impact which was hardly to be expected.

> Robin Thornber, *The Guardian*, 12 Mar. 1975

Taking what seemed to me more than just a cue from Peter Brook's

Les Iks (also, remember, about a poor, remote community which had been studied at first hand by an ecological author from the western way of life), the company and its directors had collaborated with Mr. Hare to show a sort of communism being tried out not as an aggressor's totalitarian regime but as an alternative to anarchy. . . . Any tendentiousness disappeared in the apparently sincere effort to show things as they were in a village learning to govern itself thirty years ago.

Eric Shorter, 'Regions',
Drama, Summer 1975, p. 62

As the only Chinese word in a script otherwise composed in good plain English it takes on mystical overtones as the evening proceeds. The Party becomes revered as the organization that gave the people Fanshen: now and everlastingly. And it comes as no surprise (though still something of a culture-shock) to hear one conscience-stricken recalcitrant lamenting his probable fate: 'I'll be thrown out of the Party — that's worse than being dead.' In one sense this is political drama of a rigour we rarely experience. . . .

Hare offers no authorial comment on the struggle, merely the assurance that it is worth waging — an assurance made explicit in the very last speech and implicit in his devoting three hours of dramatic time to it. Granted that these hours are informative and occasionally gripping, doubts arise. 'Under the Communists too many meetings'; so many that one wonders what time could be found actually to work the land so exhaustively discussed. Perhaps this is simply a reflection of what can and cannot be efficiently represented on a stage. But its effect is to provide both for the presenters and the audience a major exercise in wish-fulfilment; there is (especially if you actually live in an urban industrial society) more fun and more intellectual glamour in discussing agrarian activity, revolutionary or otherwise, than in actually performing it. Politics, divorced from any visible effect other than the humiliation of an unpleasant landlord or two, becomes an end in itself.

Robert Cushman, 'Bertolt Out-Brechted',
The Observer, 4 May 1975

Those who demand easy messages will be baffled by *Fanshen*: to others it will seem something very close to an austere masterpiece of political theatre.

Harold Hobson, *Sunday Times*, 27 April 1975

The drama is in the dialectics. For generations the peasants lined the pockets — and larders — of the landlords, whose power went unquestioned. Why? they are finally forced to ask. Because the landlords own the land and the peasants need the landlords' land in order to live. Did they ever think that the landlords equally depend on them — on their work? Suddenly they are made to question who needs whom, who depends on whom, for what and why. The peasants are taught to accept nothing at face value, to question everything until it makes sense, or until they can change it so that it does make sense. The play charts the process of change — the liberating ups and the many difficult downs. The first change is a redistribution of the wealth: but how do you do it? What is fair? What is equal? . . .

The dialectics — workers trying to work out a workable system — are truly fascinating, and the issues are neither over-simplified nor sentimentalized. *Fanshen* is not a polemic, but an attempt to present a particular process objectively. [The directors] use a variety of Brechtian distancing devices — white lighting, direct address, actors commenting on characters, spoken placards — to avoid subjective distortions. There were few concessions to bourgeois form in the play, and few in the style of production. . . . I also wondered how relevant the Long Bow revolutionary process was to a modern industrial society. The process of the play applied to Russia in 1917, to China in 1946, and to Cuba in 1959, but how does it apply to England now? If a factory worker or even a suburban executive wanted to fanshen, how would he go about it? As I say, it makes you think.

Catherine Itzin, 'Dramatic Dialectics to Make You Think',
Tribune, 9 May 1975, p. 7

See also:

Bert Cardullo, 'Brecht and *Fanshen*', *Studia Neophilologica*, LVIII, 1986, p. 225-30.

Bert Cardullo, '*Fanshen*, Western Drama, and David Hare's Oeuvre', *San Jose Studies*, X, Spring 1984, p. 31-41.

Michael Coveney, 'Turning over a New Life', *Plays and Players*, June 1975, p. 10-13. [Interviews with Gaskill and Stafford-Clark about the play.]

Teeth 'n' Smiles

A play in two acts, with lyrics by Tony Bicât and music by Nick Bicât.

First production: Royal Court Th., 2 Sept. 1975 (dir. Hare; with Helen
   Mirren as Maggie, Jack Shepherd as Arthur, Dave King as Saraffian,
   Cherie Lunghi as Laura, and Antony Sher as Anson).
Revived: Wyndham's Th., 26 May 1976 (cast changes: Martin Shaw as
   Arthur and Gay Hamilton as Laura).
First U.S. production: Folger Th. Group, Washington, 12 Oct. 1977
   (dir. Jonathan Alper and Louis W. Scheeder).
Published: Faber, 1976.

---

*Set on the night of 9 June 1969, when a rock group is perform-
ing at the May Ball at Jesus College, Cambridge. Maggie, the
lead vocalist, is becoming a despairing alcoholic. Saraffian, the
manager, has some sympathy for the people he has hoped to
cash in on (and with), and more for assets which can be
capitalized — which the group has proved not to be. Arthur, the
songwriter, is torn between the dreams represented by the
group, which have evaporated, and his more conventional
background. The musicians quarrel, they are charged with
possessing drugs, and Maggie burns down the wine tent. The
final song is 'Last Orders on the* Titanic' : *'The ship is
sinking / But the music remains the same'.*

I'd been writing about figures in public life and people who were far
removed from me and everyone kept saying, why does your generation
of writers never write about yourselves, why do you always batten on
the weaknesses of other generations or go back into history to exploit the
general decadence of other ways of life. But it takes a long time to assimi-
late autobiographical experience. If you write about something directly
within your own experience, as this play is, then it's best to do it eight
years on. It's just taken that long to get the perspective I wanted on that
particular series of events. . . . I think it's so boring and dishonest when
writers dress up their own experience. They think that by changing a few
details they distance themselves. . . . So I thought, if you were going to
write about something you'd experienced, it was much better to be
honest and not change *any* of the critical details. Like I *did* go to Jesus
College, Cambridge, and there *were* rock groups visiting at the time.
Everything on the surface is documentarily accurate. The rock groups
were fantastically aggressive and they hated having to play those dates,
and they were extremely rude to the audience, and by and large their
audiences disliked them very much too. It was an extraordinary clash of
two worlds: these May balls with people dressed up and performing a

complete parody of a life that was over many, many years ago, and into that crashed these rock bands, like travelling trouble on the move. . . .

There is this wonderful comedy of rock musicians. It *is* intrinsically very, very funny that so many rock musicians are so pretentious and so thick and they lead such bloody awful lives that they just go catatonic with the sheer exhaustion and exploitation. There's that side to it and then there's the other side that they *are* often very good musicians and they *do* just live through their music. They feel that having played their music that their music says everything that they have to say. But the other side of their lives has this funny numb quality about it. Words have a numb value. Deliberately through the play you see completely spaced out characters and you can't believe that they can actually get a sentence out but they leap up, pick up a bass guitar and are so completely transformed when they hit the stage. In many ways the play is about whether talking has any point at all. There are the bands who believe in music and keep saying things like 'it's not worth discussing' and there are the figures like Arthur the songwriter and Anson the student who believe in articulating things and these two worlds jam together as they did in the 'sixties, and they do in the play. . . .

Suddenly I was very struck with the thought of somebody [like Maggie] living a life in which they avoided all opportunities of being happy. It wasn't that they couldn't find themselves, or relate, or any of those boring things that people said in the 'fifties and 'sixties, it was because they were actually frightened of being happy because they felt it was wrong. I think this is a fact about living in the West, in this part of the century. People are conscious of the absurdly over-privileged lives they've led, that nothing has ever been really difficult for them. . . . The characters in the play either believe protective things; that's to say they surround themselves with zen or with the belief in the class war, or a belief in art, and they say inside my skull I've got the whole world worked out but of course there's nothing I can do about what's going on outside. Or like Maggie, they try for pure action which just moves you on into the next square.

Hare, interviewed by Ann McFerran, 'End of the Acid Era',
Time Out, 29 Aug. 1975, p. 15

In *Teeth 'n' Smiles* a girl chooses to go to prison because it will give her an experience of suffering which is bound in her eyes to be more worthwhile than the life she could lead outside: not one English critic could bring himself to mention this central event in the play, its plausibility, its implications. It was beyond their scope to engage with such an idea.

Hare, 'A Lecture Given at King's College, Cambridge',
Licking Hitler, p. 68

Tawny-maned, full-fleshed, the woman kneels keening in a bright pool of light. Suddenly out of the dark around her snout-faces glimmer, a worshipful, gruff, despairing chorus — and as suddenly vanish into limbo. She is Circe with her brutalized crew; she is also Maggie, small-time rock singer falling apart in a world of drink and drugs and tiny talents hopelessly overblown. . . . Helen Mirren has a brave shot at this lost girl. New Town bred, not very bright, not very good, in and out of alcoholic stupors yet distilling a sorry little dignity from her degradation.

J. W. Lambert, 'Breakdown and Endurance',
Sunday Times, 7 Sept. 1975

The play's main flaw is that it is as much Arthur's as Maggie's. . . . Arthur represents his emotions, and the university cleverness which has turned against itself, which makes him the more lifelike and interesting character. With his melancholy, self-mocking jokes and imitations of Astaire and Cole Porter, he almost softens Maggie's anger to a Cowardesque sigh of stylish regret at how impotent cheap music turned out to be. . . . Everyone in the play is a little too clever, too funny, too articulate, to be true. Even the group's stone-hearted manager Saraffian turns out, in Dave King's beautifully understated performance, to be a shrewd, self-loathing epigrammatist whose class-hatred has been undermined by a taste for vintage ports and vintage futilities. The evening works too well as theatre, allows itself too much dazzle and enjoyment, to put over satisfactorily the serious point it is trying to make. . . .

Teeth 'n' Smiles is about the challenge of pop music in the 'sixties to the way privilege has re-grouped itself in Britain since 1945: to the citadels of meritocracy, the playing-fields of competitive education, the boys and girls from good, book-lined homes who climb effortlessly from grammar school to Oxbridge to the executive jobs advertised, alongside Heal's furniture and the latest biography of Virginia Woolf, in the columns of the *Sunday Times*.

Ronald Bryden, *Plays and Players*, Nov. 1975, p. 21-2

Much of its appeal is that of a backstage musical with superior dialogue; we watch the musicians before, between, and after sets and enjoy their reactions — a mixture of incredulity and derision — to the surroundings in which their manager has landed them. Their weariness breeds wit; Mr. Hare has a dashing way with one-liners and a rarer gift for building a gag over a period. . . . The band are apt to remark caustically that [Maggie's misery] is no more than a pose that has got into the bone, and Mr. Hare seems three-quarters inclined to agree with them. Alternately crying up Maggie's anguish and laughing it down, he ends up with what he probably most wants to avoid: sentimentality. . . . The band's manager makes an overlong speech about a wartime bomb in the Café de Paris from which he finally draws a moral about the persistence of the class war. This, Maggie points out, is an idea that has for years saved him the risk and effort of action; but if she has an idea or a plan of action of her own she never lets on. . . .

Occasionally a line like 'the acid dream is over' suggests that we are in at the end of an era; 1969 was, no argument, the end of the 'sixties but *Teeth 'n' Smiles*, unlike *Kennedy's Children* [by Robert Patrick], cannot make this appear of more than statistical significance. Towards the close the play goes strident and a touch didactic as if Mr. Hare were trying to force us and himself into seeing a meaning. . . . The lack of confrontation between rock and Cambridge is fair enough; rock presents no challenge and Cambridge is hardly present. . . . There are moments in the play when the confrontation is presumed to have taken place but it is best to forget these and take the evening as a celebration — almost an embodiment — of musicians' cool, a perennial and generally uncommitted thing.

Robert Cushman, 'Rocking at the Court',
The Observer, 7 Sept. 1975

As a piece of drama, it lacks the cohesiveness and inner rhythm of his last original work, *Knuckle*; but as a piece of theatre it is abundantly alive and should go straight to the heart of a generation hovering uneasily between youth and early middle age. It is, in fact, a play about endings: about the ending of relationships, careers, dreams, and a slightly tacky segment of English culture. . . . Admittedly Hare gives us half a dozen possible endings and I was never quite clear whether he thought minor rock bands had given a new charge to somnolent English life.

Michael Billington, *The Guardian*, 3 Sept. 1975

Hare doesn't deny that the 'sixties was full of tat and mush but, exactly like Osborne in *The Entertainer*, he realizes there is poetry and pathos in the spectacle of decline. On a second viewing, the parallels with Osborne's play are very striking: a lead character (in this case, the group's drunken vocalist) who combines second-rateness with a maudlin sense of defiance, an abrasive wit, and candour that causes a few ripples of outrage amongst the theatre's more staid patrons and, above all, the ability to connect a small pocket of showbiz with the fat of England at large.

Michael Billington, *The Guardian*, 27 May 1976

35

What Mr. Hare is really on about here is not the wonderful world of Janis Joplin, nor even the sheer bloody awfulness of being a third-rate minor cult pop group. . . . What Mr. Hare is on about, through Maggie and those he puts around her, is the generation of twenty-five-year-olds who feel they're on the *Titanic* without much chance of getting it to change course. Maggie is thus not a great tragic figure: she's a girl from Stevenage who thought things might work out better. . . . The only difference between 1912 and 1943 and 1969, Mr. Hare appears to be saying, is that the bands on the *Titanic* and at the Café de Paris never had agents with the sense to start a little light looting. But in the end none of Hare's characters is waving or drowning either: just trying to make up their minds about the depth and temperature of the water.

Sheridan Morley, *Shooting Stars* (London, 1983), p. 25-6

See also:

John Russell Brown, *A Short Guide to Modern British Drama* (Heinemann, 1982), p. 69-70.

Licking Hitler

A play for television.
Transmitted: 'Play for Today', BBC1, 10 Jan. 1978 (dir. Hare; with Bill Paterson as Archie and Kate Nelligan as Anna).
Published: Faber, 1978; in *The History Plays*, Faber, 1984.

As the British Army moved with apparent purpose into a golden Palladian house, a ferocious Scots voice was heard dictating a speech about the flight of Rudolf Hess, and a stone-deaf old gentleman made mimic gestures of heartbreak at the bottom of the stairs. The speech grew ever more violent and disgusted, defending the Fuhrer and ending with the words 'I cry for Germany'. The old gentleman was lending his house to the war effort and departed, with the Scotsman's smiling curse, to spend the duration in Eaton Square. Clearly something unusual was about to take place. The task of what Mr. Hare described as a Research Unit of Political Warfare Executive was to undermine civilian morale in Germany by transmitting rumours in apparently overheard dialogue — more casual, and therefore more plausible, than conventional propaganda. The unit's most inventive writer was Archie MacLean, a hard-drinking hack who had fought his way into Fleet Street from the Red Clyde: Archie's peculiarly manic talents were believed to excuse his appalling behaviour by all the frightfully well-bred people in the unit except Anna. Mr. Hare being a playwright first and an historian of English social attitudes second, he made Anna — and possibly Archie — fall in love. They were Beauty and the Beast. On first arriving at the house, the genteel and finely connected Anna could not even make tea, and it was typical of the detail in Kate Nelligan's performance that we could tell instantly from the way she held her pint that she had never drunk beer before. Anna and Archie made up the play's central antithesis: past and future, old and new, south and north Britain. Archie was fighting a terrible battle to get up into the light; Anna had been up there all the time without ever knowing there was anywhere else. Both, in other words, had everything to learn, and it was Mr. Hare's triumph to invest them lightly with all these symbols while never forgetting the anger behind Archie's wildness and the distress behind Anna's calm. Having resisted Archie's savage drunken attacks by placing a chair behind her bedroom door, Anna finally succumbed, but the only result of their 'thing' was that Anna began painfully to learn the truth while the conditioned Archie went on telling lies. Mr. Hare's only concession to slickness was to compress the rest of Anna's moral and political education into a knowing 'documentary' postscript, but, this apart, David Rose's production and Mr. Hare's own direction were impeccably in period and hypersensitive to feeling and mood.

Michael Ratcliffe, *The Times*, 11 Jan. 1978

[Sefton Delmer's *Black Boomerang*] provided the factual basis for *Licking Hitler*. . . . Wise friends have told me that I should have left the metaphor alone, and that the last part of the film in which I bring the lives of the central characters up to date is the weakest. It is certainly the clumsiest in execution, and, given the chance again, I would stomp through the years with less heavy boots. But I cannot concede that the intention was wrong. To me the story is not finished until you see that years later both Anna Seaton and Archie Maclean are trapped in myths about their own past from which they seem unwilling to escape. This theme serves me again in *Plenty*, but even in *Licking Hitler* it infuriated people, who asked how I could allow so fine a heroine to grow so convincingly through her wartime experience and yet be shown years later to have become effectively a victim of it. I have got used to the clamour for a simpler morality. In the same way, feminists have been unkind to the film for its portrayal of a woman who chooses to go on meeting and making love to a man who has originally taken her by rape. They object that although such things do regrettably happen, it is the duty of responsible writers not to show them happening, and particularly via a medium which for the rest of the evening will be reinforcing the most abject sexual stereotypes. I cannot accept this argument, for to portray only what you would like to be true is the beginning of censorship. In addition Anna, however flawed, *is* the conscience of the play. . . .

Licking Hitler stirred up people's memories, and many wrote to me about their direct experience of a landscape I had only imagined. I have rarely been happier than in the days I spent before shooting when I went to interview at first hand as many of the original black propaganda teams as I could find. . . . We filmed in Compton Verney, a fine country house which had once served as a lunatic asylum. I had never looked down a camera until the first day of shooting. This was my own secret, which I only revealed later in the week.

Hare, 'Introduction', *The History Plays*, p. 13-14

When I was writing *Licking Hitler* I had Orwell in mind. Because Orwell was a radical he had to decide what he was going to do during the War. As it turned out, he didn't do that much. He said there were only three things a radical could do — accept it, endure it, or record it. And so I posed the idea of the radical in Archie who is in fact doing disgusting work. But his attitude is one of acceptance. As he says 'Just accept it; that's all you can do. I hate it, but accept it'.

Hare, interviewed by Judy Dempsey,
Literary Review, 22 Aug.-4 Sept. 1980, p. 35

What [Hare] lacks as a writer is a receptive nature. He has all the chill confidence of his generation of state-subsidized theatrical rebels, made more terrible in his case by authentic talent. . . . This time he was talking about World War II, but once again the real subject was the class war in Britain. . . . It was a fine, radical theme which was completely convincing until you reminded yourself that upper-class English girls usually *can* make tea and do a lot of other things besides. . . . The film

was stamped with authority in every department, but finally it was icy.
Clive James, The Observer, 15 Jan. 1978

Licking Hitler — the title is sickeningly ambiguous — was . . . an examination not simply of a particular time, and a special segment of war-work, but of the gangrenous nature of deception. . . . *Licking Hitler* cannot be safely locked away in its period and was not simply 'about' a dirty-tricks department in the embalmed 1940s. . . . *Licking Hitler* had many of the characteristics of the Black Propaganda it was examining. How often does a television programme leave one so alert and so wary?
Dennis Potter, 'Moments of Truth', Sunday Times, 15 Jan. 1978

See also:

Richard Johnstone, 'Television Drama and the People's War', *Modern Drama*, XXVIII, June 1985, p. 189-97 [also on Ian McEwan's *The Imitation Game* and Trevor Griffiths's *Country*].

Deeds

A two-act play, written with Howard Brenton, Ken Campbell and Trevor Griffiths.
First production: Nottingham Playhouse, 9 Mar. 1978 (dir. Richard Eyre).
Published: Plays and Players, May 1978, p. 41-50; June 1978, p. 43-50.

A modern Candide in twenty scenes that include the lobby of the House of Commons, a bathroom at the Savoy, Speakers' Corner, a prison yard, a lift, and a tanker filled with baby milk. The play, in fact, takes the form of quest. A working-class man's baby dies in hospital. Cause of death: dehydration. But he refuses to accept this explanation and so searches through society for the why and how. A nurse drops a hint of a baby food that has been wrongly mixed. And so the hero scatters the contaminated product through a Manchester supermarket, does time, lobbies MPs and Ministers to get it banned, attacks its manufacturers and immerses himself in a tankful of the stuff. At the end he and his wife decide to call their next baby either

Geronimo or Boadicea: a sign that the weapon of aggression will be handed on to the next generation. . . . The real test of its strength, as Shaw said of A Doll's House, *will be the work it does in the world.*

Michael Billington, *The Guardian*, 11 Mar. 1978

There are belligerent, bewildered passages that suggest Brenton, others with a northern wit that could be Griffiths. Underneath everything is a wild anger, not exempt from sentimentality, that could be anybody's except, curiously, Griffiths's; his rages are generally more practical. Nor is he usually given, though most of his contemporaries are, to the profusion of incident that marks this play. . . . The best recent political plays have explored a specific issue and let it reverberate. *Deeds* skips the issue and jumps to the reverberations which, accordingly, do not reverb; I doubt if any of the collaborators would have worked so sloppily on his own.

Robert Cushman, 'Mr. Deeds Goes to Prison', *The Observer*, 19 Mar. 1978

The tone of the writing is as variable as one would expect in a collective text. At one extreme, it touches anarchic comedy in a Speakers' Corner scene dominated by an anti-plastics millenarian ('you're not wearing that plastic mac: it's wearing you!'); at the other, it inhabits a region of grief and desolation. . . . For all its variety of tone and divided authorship, the play amounts to an enraged scream of pain from someone at the bottom of the social heap against the forces that allegedly control our lives: hospitals, MPs, police, giant corporations. One can sympathize with that, but not with the authors' readiness to substitute hatred and contempt for enlightenment.

Irving Wardle, 'Fighting the System', *The Times*, 11 Mar. 1978

See also:

Gareth and Barbara Lloyd Evans, eds., *Plays in Review, 1956-1980* (Batsford, 1985), p. 228-9.

Plenty

A play in two acts.

First production: Lyttelton Th., 7 Apr. 1978 (dir. Hare; with Kate
   Nelligan as Susan, Stephen Moore as Raymond Brock, and
   Julie Covington as Alice).
First U.S. production: Arena Stage, Washington, 4 Apr. 1980.
First New York production: New York Shakespeare Festival at Public
   Newman Th., 21 Oct. 1982 (dir. Hare; with Kate Nelligan as Susan,
   Edward Hermann as Raymond Brock, and Ellen Parker as Alice).
Film: released 1985, script by Hare (dir. Fred Schepisi; with Meryl
   Streep as Susan, Charles Dance as Raymond Brock, Tracey Ullman
   as Alice, John Gielgud as Sir Leonard Darwin, Ian McKellen as Sir
   Andrew Charleson, and Sting as Mick).
Published: Faber, 1978, with a two-page 'Note on Performance' by
   Hare; in *The History Plays*, Faber 1984.

*The protagonist is Susan Traherne, who at the age of seventeen
was in British intelligence, serving in occupied France during
the Second World War. But we first meet her in 1962, in the first
of the play's twelve scenes, after her mind and spirit have been
battered by what has happened to her since the war. Thus Hare
ensures an acrid tone under Scene Two when we move back nine-
teen years to wartime France, where Susan is aiding a British
agent who has just landed by parachute — a Susan who is clear-
headed, courageously frightened, tensely radiant with the
pleasure of being useful and used. The rest of the play journeys
ahead to 1962, dramatizing with bitterness and bitter wit how
Susan came to be the disturbed, desperate woman that she is.
The very last scene returns to France, Susan on a hilltop with a
French farmer on the day of liberation in 1944. Joyfully she
says, 'There will be days and days and days like this', the last
line of a play that has just blackly contradicted this last line. We
have seen Susan move on a descending pilgrimage, through an
affair with a former intelligence colleague which was apparently an attempt to keep in touch with a companion of the war
days; through an affair with a Foreign Office attaché that turns
into a strained marriage; through a cool (and unsuccessful)
arrangement with another man to father a child; and, possibly
trying to sublimate frustration about this failure, through a
sorry attempt with a Foreign Office chief to improve her
husband's career. (The theme of the Foreign Office runs
through the play like the ghost of former British power; also, the*

*very idea of service, bureaucratic though it may be, has a grip
on Susan's sensibility. The one heroic character in the play is a
former British ambassador who resigns in disgust over British
behaviour at Suez in 1956 and dies soon after.) Susan's own
life, in advertising before marriage and in frustrating idleness
afterward, unravels: brings her close to mental collapse.
Because of her interference at the Foreign Office, her husband
has been forced to leave the government; he has gone into
insurance, is doing all right, is still devoted. But her post-war
disappointments in herself and in the world finally boil up into
quarrels between the pair. . . . Hare counterpoises Susan with a
friend named Alice whose life wobbles a bit at the start but who
rights herself with socially contributory work.*

Stanley Kauffmann, *Theater Criticisms*
(New York: Performing Arts Journal Publications, 1983), p. 162-5,
reprinted from *Saturday Review*, March 1983

It is a common criticism of my work that I write about women whom I
find admirable, but whom the audience dislikes. The truth is more
complicated than that, but it is true that large sections of an English
audience, particularly the men, are predisposed to find Susan Traherne
unsympathetic. . . . I planned a play in twelve scenes, in which there
would be twelve dramatic actions. Each of these actions is intended to
be ambiguous, and it is up to the audience to decide what they feel about
each event. For example, in Scene Three, there will be some who feel
that Susan does the kindest possible thing in sparing her lover's wife the
knowledge of the circumstances of his death; but others may feel that the
manner in which she disposes of the corpse is a little heartless. Again, in
Scene Four you may feel that the way she gets rid of her boyfriend is
stylish, and almost exemplary in its lack of hurtfulness; or you may feel
it is crude and dishonest. This ambiguity is central to the idea of the
play. The audience is asked to make its own mind up about each of the
actions. In the act of judging, the audience learns something about its
own values. It is therefore important that a balance of sympathy is
maintained throughout the evening, and that the actress playing Susan
puts the case for her as strongly as she can. The case against her makes
itself, or is made by the other characters. . . .

The time-scheme of the play is not as intimidating to audiences as it
at first appears. Clues are built into each scene to tell you where you are,
and how many years have passed. . . . Alice is intended to be a
historically accurate character, a bohemian of the late 'forties, part of
whose charm must in retrospect seem to be her innocence. The path of

dissent which she takes is very different from Susan's because it is mostly sexual. By the end of the play she is mellow, but stranded. Brock, on the other hand, has sold out, but, crucially, is intelligent enough to know that he has. . . . To those of you who perform the play abroad, I can only say that its Englishness is of the essence. . . . Irony is central to English humour, and as a people we are cruel to each other, but always quietly.

> Hare, 'A Note on Performance', *Plenty* (1978), p. 87-8

Plenty is inspired by a belief that people died literally in vain. That the upsurge of radical feeling was a genuine outcome of their experiences and not an accident, that the material and emotional plenty of that last period of affluence was wasted, and that the British have drawn a mantle of lies and coldness over the war. We are afraid to show our emotions.

> Hare, interviewed by Steve Grant, 'Peace and *Plenty*',
> *Time Out*, 7 Apr. 1978, p. 15

What drives Susan mad is that society doesn't offer any good way to live. *Plenty* is about the cost of a life spent in dissent, which is the common experience of thinking people in England. We don't like our society, we feel ill at ease, we're constantly upset. The play is about that, and also about the strength of the institutions we have to work in. I wanted to write about something very common in England, of making the past run your life. . . . The great criticism of Susan is that she becomes obsessed with what happened in the war, and it doesn't help her in the peace.

> Hare, interviewed by Benedict Nightingale,
> 'An Angry Young Briton of the Eighties Brings his Play to New York',
> *New York Times*, 17 Oct. 1982, Sec. II, p. 1, 6

I had originally been attracted by a statistic, which I now cannot place, that 75 per cent of the women flown behind the lines for the Special Operations Executive were subsequently divorced after the war. The person who has had a good war and then can find no role in the peace is, of course, a character who has often been written before. . . . I also had the wider aim of trying to set one character's life against the days of English plenty. In England the opposition to *Plenty* forms around the feeling that from the start Susan Traherne contains the seeds of her own destruction, and that the texture of the society in which she happens to live is nearly irrelevant, for she is bent on objecting to it, whatever its qualities. This was certainly not what I intended, yet I can see that in the

English theatre the counter-balance of the play, which is Brock's destruction, does go comparatively unremarked because it is the kind of death so many members of the audience have chosen, a death by compromise and absorption into institutional life. I intend to show the struggle of a heroine against a deceitful and emotionally stultified class, yet some sections of the English audience miss this, for they see what Susan is up against as life itself. . . . The play proved to be a lot less controversial in America and enjoyed a breadth of approval which I had never known at home. In part this was no doubt because the American audience felt themselves much less implicated in the play's judgements. . . . They were also, of course, not afraid to look English society in the eye, to see Suez as criminal and the Foreign Office as absurd. They also seemed less frightened of a strong woman.

Hare, 'Introduction', *The History Plays*, p. 15-16

I stopped admiring the woman. I really wanted to pummel her. I would come to the middle of the second act, and I would just withdraw my consent from that woman. I don't think the audience ever knew, but I was very worried about it.

Kate Nelligan on Susan, quoted by Urjo Kareda,
'Nelligan's Leaps', *Saturday Night* (Toronto), Aug. 1985, p. 27

For those with the self-confidence to practice it, a good rule when unable to guess what a play is about is to assume that it is not about anything. The suspicion will often prove to be well-founded, and even if the author denies it, it is only his word against yours. . . . What does the author want us to think, to feel? What is he saying? What does he believe about his characters and their predicament? There is no telling, and it is no use searching the title for clues, either, for it has less discernible connection with the contents than in any play since *Twelfth Night*. . . . I believe that *Plenty* is about its plot, which is never actually uninteresting, but leads nowhere in particular. If Mr. Hare believes it is about something more, and leads somewhere definite, well, I suppose he is entitled to his opinion.

Bernard Levin, *Sunday Times*, 16 Apr. 1978

Plenty is a political play with the politics left out. The audience has to do some heavy inferring to perceive that the lost chance for change through radical politics is central in the morass of Susan's disappointments. Clausewitz said that war is the continuation of politics by other means; *Plenty* would be even better than it is, would be complete, if it showed

Susan realizing the reverse of Clausewitz's dictum — that peace is a means of continuing the politics that were heightened by war. Even if her political struggle had failed, it would have taken her collapse deeper than self-centredness and would have put the thematic base of the play more closely in key with the acerbic dialogue.

Stanley Kauffmann, Theater Criticisms, p. 164

Plenty is a cry of disgust with Britain — with the wet, the cold, the flu, the food, the loveless English — and with the horror of sexual repression, the futility of sexual freedom, the corruption of wealth, the lie of good behaviour, the decay of belief, the deceit of advertising, the hell of suburban marriage, the pettiness of life in the corporate bureaucracy and the indignity of death. I think we can say that David Hare has had a bellyful, like Osborne, and again like him he compares the desolate present with a nobler and more heroic past. . . .

The cinematic construction, in twelve scenes that keep the action hurtling forward, or backward and forward, gives a feeling of hectic development that never quite becomes organic growth; and the feeling is intensified by the inclusion of some sketchy minor characters, such as the schoolgirl who wants an abortion and a Burmese couple who might have stepped in from a television series about our Asian friends. Watching it come down, I felt as confused as the play itself is. It may mean more to those for whom Suez still rings a bell. But what bell? The play expresses a disenchantment with a post-imperial England which itself seems historically remote. The period is '43 to '62, but it's crammed with prochronisms, not only in the language, but in the casual references to sex, drugs, and battered wives. . . . *Plenty* condemns the English for refusing to turn over and for evidently preferring materialism and a hierarchical order. Unfortunately it skips the political analysis that might explain that preference, and is reduced to railing against the nation's stupidity and celebrating its own intelligence. . . . Beneath the glacially witty dialogue of his play is a dangerous nostalgia and deep sense of exhaustion, with a patrician-romantic distaste that is thoroughly English in tone.

Ted Whitehead, 'North of Suez',
The Spectator, 22 Apr. 1978

The one quality missing (or deliberately repressed) is amplitude: everything is filed down, reduced to gritty essentials, with the exception of the occasional climax such as the husband's frenzied outburst after fifteen years of marital torment. One casualty of this discipline is the sense of connection between the public and the private stories: which, in themselves, are curiously fragmentary. The details Mr. Hare supplies do not accumulate into a portrait of post-war Britain, even with the help of Victor Sylvester and snide digs at the Third Programme. Likewise, Susan's career leaves a string of unanswered questions: why, as a self-professed solitary, does she need the constant companionship of her girl-friend, Alice, a messy would-be writer who sponges on her and disrupts her? Why, again, does she make her disastrous Civil Service marriage (after it is on the rocks, Mr. Hare admittedly does offer a flimsy explanation)? What precisely is driving her round the bend in the final scenes? Those are plot questions: but from moment to moment you are left unprepared for her next arbitrary act and destructive line. Mr. Hare, it is true, specializes in shocks rather than preparation, and some of them are extremely powerful.

Irving Wardle,
The Times, 13 Apr. 1978

By relating Susan's experience to major historical events, Hare is able to suggest that her disillusion is representative rather than merely individual, and thus the play becomes a form of social commentary as it examines the general as well as the particular causes of Susan's problem. The chief target for attack is not, however, the entire social and political system, it is the British characteristic of emotional reserve, the repression of feelings. Sir Leonard Darwin is afforded a certain respect in the play, because, however outdated his reasons, he expresses his outrage at the time of Suez over the government's failure to keep the Civil Service informed. It is the common lack of such courage, the general refusal to give vent to one's feelings and speak one's mind, that is implicitly suggested to be the cause of the stagnation in society which is at the root of Susan's pain. Susan herself, though quite prepared to let go and certainly not lacking the courage of her convictions, is never-theless inhibited because there is nowhere she can direct her energy when surrounded by people who stoically accept their situation. As she herself remarks, 'I'd like to change everything but I don't know how'. . . . The play is so firmly located in the disappointment of hopes aroused by the end of the war that it lacks immediacy to our present situation. . . . The lack of stridency in *Plenty*, its implicit rather than overtly argued social comment, have led some critics to conclude that it lacks substance and has nothing to say. This is pure laziness on their behalf, but it demonstrates the extent to which Hare refuses to prescribe cures for the problems he highlights. His plays are refresh-ingly understated for modern social and political drama. They cannot be reduced to a simple message, for his characters are not manipulated simply to prove a thesis. The power of his work is to provoke thought and disturb complacency. Certainly the study of suffering and waste in *Plenty* does no less than that.

Colin Ludlow, *London Magazine*, July 1978, p. 76-8

The most interesting question for the audience is whether Susan is a strong-willed dissenter, a monstrous destroyer, or a pathetic madwoman. . . . What unnerves Susan, apparently, is the mediocrity and stupidity of everyone around her. *Plenty* is a metaphor for post-war England. It's the story of how Britain in decline made a fool of itself, especially over Suez. . . . But can anyone believe that if it weren't for the decay of British society Susan would be a nice, happy person?

Martin Knelman, 'Top Girl',
Saturday Night (Toronto), Apr. 1983, p. 67-8

From petty ambassadorial betrayals to the infinitely greater treachery of Suez, Mr. Hare charts a nation in decline: writing like some latter-day Rattigan crossed with Charles Addams, he produces as playwright and director a black comedy so stylish, so acidly funny, and so broad in its measure that we end up with an epic of disillusion and articulate rage. In defining the gradual disintegration and reformation of one lady's spirit, Hare's message is that power rots but money rots faster: his world is one where it has taken 6,000 civil servants to dismantle an Empire built by 600, and where an ex-Embassy staffer (Stephen Moore at his most hesitantly urbane) can look back in nostalgia because 'say what you like about the Foreign Office, at least they were hypocrites; in the City they don't even try that'. Mr. Hare's message, sent back from the outer reaches of disillusion, is that finally the only dignity lies in being alone, since together we've managed to ruin even twenty years of peace. A national failure of guts and truth is what Mr. Hare is on about here, and he writes with a coherent and committed though well-controlled rage.

Sheridan Morley, *Shooting Stars* (1983), p. 130-1,
reprinted from *Punch*

On the film of *Plenty*

Hare's script for the film differs substantially from the stage play, with the scenes arranged chronologically. Changes include a sex-and-love encounter with Lazar at the start in wartime France, the elimination of Dorcas and Louise, and the Festival of Britain (1951) episode moved to the Coronation (1953).

47

Meryl's performance [as Susan] draws the audience in — she has a great gift for playing uncommon women in a way that everybody can understand and appreciate. That's an incredible talent. But perhaps there was more of a challenge performing the part in the theatre. A theatre performance challenges everyone in the audience. They felt, 'O, my God! This woman [Nelligan] is going to come offstage and ask something of me! Am I going to be able to do it?' In that respect, perhaps Meryl's performance is less challenging.

Hare, interviewed by Dan Yakir,
'Hare Style', *Horizon*, Dec. 1985, p. 46

In my desire to freshen, I threw out much of the play. It was Meryl who insisted on restoring big chunks; I remember her saying: 'What's remarkable about Susan is not so much what she felt, but how she expressed it'. Meryl wanted to have those speeches, those pieces of eloquence. So the whole rehearsal period involved striking a balance between the play and the new, epic style Fred was eager to implement in the film. . . . Onstage, *Plenty* was organized by scene and focused on the development of a character. On film, we had the chance for more narrative drive and could show a lot of history — the Coronation sequence, for example. In terms of visualizing twenty years of a woman's life, film can be much purer. . . . Much of what Susan's trying to recapture goes back to one night during the war. My play *Licking Hitler* suggested this, too — that sex under such circumstances has a special charge. In the theatre you have to do it with words; language is a kind of surrogate. And I think this scene makes their reunion in the seaside hotel that much more powerful. . . . In the play, the character of Alice was a witness, but she trailed away. In the film, Alice's disillusionment with men is a strong counterpoint to Susan; it liberates her to bring Susan back from Jordan.

Hare, interviewed by Steve Lawson, 'Hare Apparent',
Film Comment, Sept.-Oct. 1985, p. 22

Theatrical contrivance shows through. He has a scattergun technique with his polemics, and requires this tiresome woman to keep taking on ludicrous jobs such as organizing upper-crust Coronation tea parties or writing dogfood commercials in order to demonstrate how appalling it all is. . . . *Plenty*, albeit well dressed, entertaining, and cleverly written, is ultimately so shallow it might as well have been called Empty.

George Perry, 'Plenty of Nothing', *Sunday Times*, 24 Nov. 1985

At the National Theatre in 1978, directed by its author, David Hare's *Plenty* seemed an ambitious, muddled failure with an astringent, even rebarbative central performance from Kate Nelligan. . . . Now as a realistic film . . . *Plenty* seems sentimental, overblown, and phoney, infinitely inferior as a social chronicle to Coward's *Cavalcade*, less authentic a picture of British life than *Mrs. Miniver*, and featuring a monotonous, oddly blank performance by Meryl Streep. . . . As a portrait of a chronic malcontent, *Plenty* is uninteresting. As the case history of a deeply disturbed woman it is inadequately documented.

> Philip French, 'False Portrait of Post-War Britain',
> *The Observer*, 24 Nov. 1985

It is suffused by that wordiness which is permissible on stage but which on the screen creates a false rhythm. When Susan declares that 'I think of France more than I can tell you', or that 'a shipping office is very important to me. I do find the work fulfilling', one might as well be listening to a news agency report. . . . *Plenty* displays no real sense of period. It is meticulous enough in its detail — perhaps too meticulous, since it suffers from the delusion that everything in a late 'forties sitting-room, for example, would actually have been made in the late 'forties — but there is no real historical imagination in evidence.

> Peter Ackroyd, 'Plenty of Nothing',
> *The Spectator*, 30 Nov. 1985, p. 39

The 1978 stage production presented a challenging, ambiguous study of how people cope with the aftermath of wartime experience, and the impoverishment of English values. . . . The tenor of the film is appreciably different, its emphasis on stylishness often enhances its ironic title, but it has lost the dark claustrophobia of the play, and at over two hours' running-time the business seems less intense. . . . As well as being a political piece (in places still rather heavy-handedly so), *Plenty* is also a love-story, and the turbulent relationship between Susan and her diplomat husband is the crucial one if an equilibrium of sympathy is to be achieved.

> David Profumo, 'Diplomatic Disaffection',
> *Times Literary Supplement*, 13 Dec. 1985

No one with any serious hopes for contemporary British writing can ignore him, yet what the devil is the chap saying about us? That we are a nation riddled with a snobbery and class-consciousness which two world wars have done nothing to shake; that, on the contrary post-war 'levelling' has enabled qualities endemic to the ruling classes, such as hypocrisy, shallow feeling, greed, idleness, and irresponsibility, to be spread more evenly lower down the social scale; that power is what an elite is excited by, and that as the elite loses its identity, or fears for its integrity, or suspects interlopers, then the fight for a hold on that power becomes ever more vicious.

Gavin Millar, 'The Habit of Lying',
Sight and Sound, Autumn 1985, p. 299

See also:

Robert Brustein, *Who Needs Theatre* (New York: Atlantic Monthly Press, 1987), p. 191-3.

Gareth and Barbara Lloyd Evans, eds., *Plays in Review, 1956-1980* (Batsford, 1985), p. 229-31.

Steven H. Gale, 'Sex and Politics: David Hare's *Plenty*', in *Drama, Sex and Politics: Themes in Drama, 7*, ed. James Redmond (Cambridge University Press, 1985), p. 213-20.

Gordon Rogoff, *Theatre is Not Safe* (Evanston, Ill.: Northwestern University Press, 1987), p. 235-7.

Dreams of Leaving

One-hour television play.
Transmitted: 'Play for Today', BBC1, 17 Jan. 1980 (dir. Hare; with Kate Nelligan as Caroline and Bill Nighy as William).
Published: Faber, 1979.

It was certainly, as advertised, a change of pace, mood, preoccupation, from Licking Hitler *and others that have come before, generally tagged as having public themes. You could scarcely get more private than* Dreams of Leaving . . . *a story of obsessive young love. William — played with accurately appalling innocence by Bill Nighy — is the new boy in the big city, his main object to pull the birds until he meets the svelte, enigmatic Caroline, and throws all away for the hope of getting a response. Well, she says she loves him as none other. But she is a manipulator, refusing him the reward — not just in bed, though she's had many and claims to lust for him, but in most other emotional ways. No wonder the lad gets knotted up and denounces his Fleet Street colleagues for doing a rotten job. . . . In the end, and it is not without its power, she is made mad. She ends, hair now pulled plainly back, in an institution. And he, shockingly, says: 'I was grateful. Thank God, she was mad.' It hadn't been him.*

Peter Fiddick, *The Guardian*, 18 Jan. 1980

If you've written a long time about social and political things you're aware that the question of who sleeps with whom is of more interest and daily currency than the state of the economy or the decline of the West. This film is an attempt to put something serious about sex on television. There's a lot of smut on television but hardly anything about the real variety of people's sexuality. I wanted to write something which a mass audience would recognize as a situation in which they'd been. And to deal with the impact of sex on people's lives. . . . It's partly about the appalling intimacy of people's real desires compared with how they actually live and about the way with sex all the normal rules are broken. . . . At the end I'll be perfectly happy if people think to themselves 'it may not say anything but it's true'.

Hare, interviewed by Michael Billington, 'Broken Rules',
Radio Times, 12 Jan. 1980, p. 17

What I'm writing about in this play and in the plays of this period are about those people who are forced to live together in cities and those people who have a selfconsciousness about themselves and who feel that 'well, we have money and we're intelligent but certainly unhappy'. The play is about the fact that you cannot run away once you attain selfconsciousness. William tries to run away. He ends up settling for a woman he doesn't really love and for children he doesn't really want. . . . Caroline is not altogether somebody I admire, that is to say she knows it's a slum life but she isn't actually doing anything about it.

Hare, interviewed by Judy Dempsey, *Literary Review*,
22 Aug. 1980, p. 35

The true mood of the play lay not in its slightly artificial literariness, still less in its Fleet Street background, but in its desolation and the power of its everyday speech, whose rhythms Miss Nelligan perceived and phrased like a singer.

Michael Ratcliffe, 'Capturing the Music of the Sphinx',
The Times, 18 Jan 1980

Dreams of Leaving has the confined simplicity and elegance of an Eric Rohmer moral tale. . . . The film is a disappointment, all the more frustrating for being so tantalizing, for offering elements that are never quite connected. . . . The public world intrudes at every point in this non-love affair — the cynicism of the media, the corrupt art market, the whining narcissism of rock stars — but it remains an unassimilated backdrop. . . . . If Caroline's fasting or anorexia (which inflicts brain damage on her) is a logical extension of her detachment from life, her inability or refusal to take nourishment — at least from William — then the metaphor seems to cry out for development, for explanation. We need to know more about her madness.

> Ian McEwan, 'Getting out and Copping out',
> *Times Literary Supplement*, 25 Jan. 1980

A Map of the World

A play in two acts. (The title comes from Oscar Wilde: 'A map of the world which does not include Utopia is not worth even glancing at.')

First production: commissioned for Adelaide Festival, Australia, 6 Mar. 1982 (dir. Hare; with Roshan Seth as Victor Mehta and Robert Grubb as Stephen).

First London production: Lyttelton Th., 27 Jan. 1983 (dir. Hare; with Roshan Seth as Victor Mehta, Bill Nighy as Stephen, and Diana Quick as Peggy).

First U.S. production: New York Shakespeare Festival at Public/Martinson Hall, 28 Oct. 1985 (dir. Hare; with Roshan Seth as Victor Mehta, Zeljko Ivanek as Stephen, and Elizabeth McGovern as Peggy).

Published: Faber, 1983; in *The Asian Plays*, 1986.

Hare takes as hero a boyishly attractive left-wing journalist — and then suggests there is arrogance and naivety in his social criticism, due to his loneliness and discontent with himself. This is Stephen. Opposite him is set Hare's best character, a philandering Indian novelist famous for loftily witty satire of the bungling immaturity of the emergent nations. This is Mehta. The pair meet in Bombay, at a UNESCO conference on world poverty. They at once fall out over a girl, an American actress who has built a philosophy out of easy promiscuity and non-commitment. This is Peggy. By an amusing if rigged contrivance, Hare makes the success of the conference depend upon a contest for Peggy's favours. Mehta is required to tone down the savagery of his planned UNESCO speech. He refuses on learning that Stephen wants him to. Peggy proposes that the two of them argue it out. She will give herself to the winner. This squalid contract leads to a Shavian debate. The dramatic outcome: Stephen loses his life in facing the reality of his proclaimed beliefs; Mehta breaks his marriage and climbs down from his superior stance; and Peggy accepts the obligations of adulthood. The play is finally a spirited defence of idealism and an attack on its great enemies — attitudinizing do-goodery as personified by Stephen, supercilious worldliness as seen in Mehta. Either leads to a death of the heart. And the trickery? I tell you, you need to keep your wits about to follow it all. What we see happening is mainly a flashback to the past. Or else, it is a re-enactment in a film studio of a falsified version of the past, derived from a novel Mehta wrote about it all. So you get a foolish film director breaking into the action. Actors step out of their roles to comment, bitch, or fuss over clothes. All great fun. But the device is also used to explain subtleties, disentangle motives. . . . At first I thought the theatrical legerdemain too clever. But the fangs of the play's social conscience sink deep and are seen finally to have been sharpened by the dramatist's mastery of his medium.

John Barber, Daily Telegraph, 28 Jan. 1983

A Map of the World is a play which argues with itself, a play full of worries and confusion. Clumsy and disparate, it unreels in a strange and unpredictable fashion, switching styles, shifting arguments. For those who want a political play about the Third World, the long passages about fiction may seem frustrating. For the theatrically minded, the approach to character and plot development may seem perverse. . . . I was obviously trying, as best I could, to articulate arguments which are of great importance to developing countries but at whose mention people in the West feel themselves, for some reason, entitled to glaze over. . . . In an ideal production of the play, you find yourself agreeing with whoever has last spoken.

Hare, 'Introduction', The Asian Plays, p. xiii-xiv

I had spent a lot of years writing about the decline of England. It was a genre. After *Plenty*, in 1978, I felt that I had said what I wanted to say on that. . . . I suppose *A Map of the World* was written partly out of exasperation at the English resistance to seeing anything except in an English context. The minute you leave this country you become aware of how local the English fashion for right-wing ideas is. If you travel in the Third World, the belief that the liberal experiment is over seems parochial.

> Hare, interviewed by Peter Lewis,
> programme for National Theatre production, 1983

The critics . . . concentrate only on those things in the play which confirm them in their own prejudices, apparently unaware that they are themselves thereby becoming a spectacular demonstration of the play's basic argument. . . . Milton Shulman, in a generous piece in *The Standard*, notes that I give the best arguments to the right-wing figure. He does not consider that perhaps they only seem to be the best arguments to him. The reviewers also present themselves as thoroughly confused by the device in the play whereby a film is shown to be made from the original events in Bombay. . . . I have no idea if *A Map of the World* is a good play or not, I only know it has not yet been judged. . . . I still have the unfashionable belief that critics should try to see plays as they are, in their fullness, and not concentrate solely on those parts which flatter their prejudices.

> Hare, 'I Still Have the Unfashionable Belief',
> *The Guardian*, 3 Feb. 1983, p. 12

The wild variations of style are very hard. Some of it, obviously, is like a debate, and the love scenes are almost like intimate cinema scenes rather than scenes for a big theatre. With all those shifts of style, it's very hard to get the audience to join you on the switchback unless you get absolutely every shift of gear right. I think it's a formidably difficult play to direct. . . . The thrust of the argument between the central characters never really fails to engage the audience. These are terribly important arguments. . . . I liked choosing a subject that was so deliberately difficult to dramatize. And in fact, of course, once you begin to lay out what the arguments are, they are fascinating arguments to hear spoken in the theatre. One of the things that's exhilarating about the play is always that the audience find that they're interested in things they thought they weren't interested in.

> Hare, interviewed by Robert Crew,
> 'Playwright Hare Feels the Sting of Controversy',
> *Toronto Star*, 11 Feb. 1989, Sec. F, p. 3

I found that because I myself was approaching middle age, I was less keen to show that the marriage between Victor and Peggy had deteriorated six years later, that whereas she had been a delightful young thing and he a sparkling novelist, theirs would be a tyrannical marriage. I found that although Victor would never admit his faults, which were many, I couldn't make him an emotionally cruel man. . . . I find the passion and the permanent state of excitability in India attractive.

> Hare, interviewed by Joan Goodman, 'New World',
> *The Observer*, 23 Jan. 1983

Mehta is a character I rather admire for his not wanting to give way to all the ballyhoo. The price he pays is that he becomes fastidious about ideas. Smelling a bad idea is like smelling a dirty pair of socks. Horrid, vulgar ideas! He has a little portmanteau of attitudes he develops and then applies to every situation. He misses out on the sheer richness and variety of life. In *A Map of the World*, I'm trying to say that no intellectual will ever be able to organize the world in the way he wants to organize it. Life will always seep back up and spoil his sand castle.

> Hare, interviewed by Mel Gussow,
> 'David Hare: Playwright as Provocateur',
> *New York Times*, 29 Sept. 1985, p. 47

There are two plots and I've been trying to smooth them out and also work on the character of the American girl. I never really got her right. I have been trying to make the play as relentless as possible.

> Hare, interviewed by W. J. Weatherby, 'Plenty of Hare',
> *The Guardian*, 19 Oct. 1985, p. 11

There is, it would seem, nothing Mr. Hare will stop at to keep that vast stage alive with challenging ideas. Unfortunately, the ultimate effect is stultifying in the extreme. Heaven knows there is not an issue he raises that should not command our care and concern yet the manner of its delivery renders it stillborn on the senses. Conversations inflate into long contrived speeches; wry arguments implode into airless debates.

> Jack Tinker, *Daily Mail*, 28 Jan. 1983

Hare's criterion in art as in politics is: whose side are you on? Are you on the side of the Third World? Are you on the side of progress? Are you fundamentally optimistic about human beings? Do you believe in the possibility of change? If so, good. If not, he says, kindly leave the stage.

> James Fenton, *Sunday Times*, 30 Jan. 1983

The arguments are presented with cogency and wit. . . . But arguments do not make a play and Mr. Hare has added two lubricants. The first is romantic: Stephen and Victor challenge one another that the winner in a staged debate shall go to bed with Peggy, the girl they both fancy. The second is dramatic: the whole scene is being filmed from a script adapted from Victor's novel in which the events, more-or-less factual, take place.

B. A. Young, *Punch*, 3 Feb. 1983

Hare has not, I think, as some observers suggest, written a play that advocates the telling of lies in favour of some utopian 'truth'. He has instead written a very good play about communication, conscience and third world politics inside which nestles a very bad play about art and sex and sexual politics. Untheatrical it may be, but it is intellectually engaging about issues that Tom Stoppard's *The Real Thing* (with which it is bound, both in form and content, to be compared) never took past first base.

Ros Asquith, *City Limits*, 3 Feb. 1983

Both positions are made witty and convincing, but Stephen and Mehta are so completely entrenched that there can't honestly be a resolution. Stephen is handed the victory only by being the author's candidate. He speaks last and his assault on Mehta's values is perhaps more unflinchingly *personal*. There's a kind of truth in that, but on the evidence, if Mehta were to speak last, the entire play could be sabotaged. It is unquestionably a draw. And the sense of being in an audience of divided loyalties is marvellously clear. But in the last twenty minutes the play's sheer complexity begins to revolt against its apparent meaning. . . . When Stephen leaves the action, the play begins to go out of focus. . . . *A Map of the World* is rich in ideas and rigorous observations, but, despite its affirmative ending, the hidden meaning of the play is far from optimistic. It seems to say that as hard as we struggle to understand them, the great movements in the world remain in the background, a continuing tragic mystery. David Hare may no longer be consciously writing about the decline of England, but the theme is still insistently there; a kind of impotence. But if the play's complexity finally undermines it, that is also a reflection of its honesty. The very best thing one can say about *A Map of the World* is that it makes Stephen's affirmation of a radical position seem important.

Dusty Hughes, 'Tract for the Times',
Literary Review, Mar. 1983, p. 27-8

See also:

Ruby Cohn, 'Theater in Recent English Theater', *Modern Drama*, XXX, Mar. 1987, p. 1-13.

Saigon

Television film.
Transmitted: Thames TV, 30 Nov. 1983 (dir. Stephen Frears; with Judi Dench as Barbara Dean, Frederic Forrest as Bob Chesneau, and E. G. Marshall as the Ambassador).
Published: Faber, 1983; in *The Asian Plays*, 1986.

Chesneau is a Cold War warrior with a conscience who, physically and in every other way, seems to have walked straight off the set of a 'fifties B-feature, while Judi Dench's Barbara Dean is the equally conventional spinster expatriate with an elderly mother back in Bournemouth. The opening scenes in which Barbara explains (voice-over) that she has always been extremely secretive suggest that an earlier version of the script may have developed the character more fully. What actually happens is that she has an affair with Chesneau, breaks with him because she disapproves of the way the Americans are handling the war, but calls on him at the last minute when her reluctance to leave the country she has grown to love means that she can only escape with help from the Embassy. Chesneau, meanwhile, learns from his Vietnamese contacts that the Vietcong intend to push right into Saigon, but fails to carry any of the arguments with his CIA colleagues and Embassy superiors who treat his demands that they prepare to plan an evacuation as 'hysterical'. But he omits to destroy his own files, perhaps because he is too busy helping Barbara Dean, and in the undignified scramble to depart he, too, betrays those who have helped him. . . . In a sense it does not matter that the relationship between the two principals is both predictable and low key since their self-absorption is simply a mirror of the political stance of the Americans in Saigon.

Jill Forbes, *Sight and Sound*,
Winter 1983-84, p. 62-3

I tried to show that, for a lot of people, life in Saigon was heaven — for both the local bourgeoisie and the working class, this was a beautiful city which offered an attractive way of life. The Americans were too busy getting out at the time to notice it.

> Hare, interviewed by Dan Yakir, 'Hare Style',
> *Horizon*, Dec. 1985, p. 46-7

It's about living in a city where you know the end is coming, and yet you lie to yourself about the end, so I hope it's not just about Vietnam.

> Hare, interviewed by Joan Goodman, 'New World',
> *The Observer*, 23 Jan. 1983, p. 44

Hare's tragic theme is the betrayal of one nation by another and, within those final days, the betrayal of a woman by a man. Judi Dench brings the genteel fragrance of Surrey to the perspiring Eastern climes — 'England's very wet', she tells Mr. Forrest, 'it makes its greenness almost iridescent, almost indecently green'. Such lines approach the wistfulness of Alan Bennett but the script, short on incident and long on dialogue, lacks his sense of structure.

> Iain Johnstone, *Sunday Times*, 13 Nov. 1983

The first half gave us Snatched Love (or the Next Best Thing) in a War-torn Country: the soundtrack opened with 'Love is the Sweetest Thing', while a banner across a Saigon street advertised the film *Love Story*, just to grip us by the elbow. After an hour or so, however, this theme keeled over like Guy Burgess on cheap vodka, and left us with a second, equally familiar theme: Getting Out of This Hell Alive. Characters were from stock, and despite some weeks' location work in Thailand, several of the street-scenes looked as if they'd been shot with help from the local Chinese take-away. It was surprising how unsurprising most of it was.

> Julian Barnes, *The Observer*, 19 Dec. 1983

Wetherby

Film.
Released: 1985 (dir. Hare; with Vanessa Redgrave as Jean Travers,
Tim McInnery as John Morgan, Judi Dench as Marcia, and Ian Holm
as Stanley).
Published: Faber, 1985.

[Hare in Wetherby *is] shuffling the basic ingredients of a P.D. James or Francis Durbridge whodunnit in Yorkshire to probe the emotional deprivations of the bourgeois world. Hare kicks off with an edgy dinner party at the fashionable converted farm-labourer's cottage of the fifty-ish schoolteacher Jean Travers in John Braine country, that affluent corner of the West Riding, where beef and Yorkshire pud have been replaced by* coq au vin *and courgettes, and shawls have given way to Burberry scarves. An air of mystery hangs over the meal and some embarrassing incident evidently occurs when Jean and a strange young guest, John Morgan, go upstairs to fix a loose tile that is letting the rain in. It transpires that Morgan too has a tile loose. The following day he returns to tell Jean he had gate-crashed her party, and then blows out his brains over her kitchen wall. These are by no means the least credible events in* Wetherby. *This suicide involves Jean and six other people — her four other middle-aged guests (a drunken, querulous, bitchy pair of married couples, who alternately rail against Thatcher and black immigrants); the tortured Inspector Langdon from the local CID, who is set apart from the local constabulary by his university degree and his refusal to join them in guffawing over sex-magazines; and the attractive, affectless undergraduate Karen, who brutally rejected Morgan when he was a graduate student at Essex. Why was Morgan there? Why did he kill himself? Who is to blame? All is revealed in a knowing, deftly edited mosaic that interweaves the continuing narrative with flashbacks to the fateful dinner party, to a swooningly romantic affair in the early 1950s between the teenage Jean and a lower-middle-class aircraftsman doomed to die in Malaya, and to Morgan's pestering of Karen at Essex and his arrival in the Yorkshire town of Wetherby. The technique suggests Losey's* Accident. *Those familiar with Hare's excellent television film* Licking Hitler *or his over-rated stage play* Plenty *will know that the real culprit in* Wetherby *is the moral miasma the author believes has enveloped Britain since Labour betrayed the spirit of 1945 and which has become increasingly toxic with the passing of each deceitful post-war decade. Those not familiar may rapidly pick up the general drift when Morgan arrives in Wetherby with paperbacks by Nietzsche and Erich Fromm in his bag, and places them on either side of his revolver. Morgan*

spells out his message when addressing the smug dinner guests on the need to discover a world of true feeling buried beneath our moribund society. He may be a psychotic with a 'disfiguring central blackness', the film asserts, but he's at least prepared to put his gun where his mouth is.

Philip French, 'A Case of Loose Tiles',
The Observer, 10 Mar. 1985

The first draft of the film was almost completely incomprehensible. It free-associated between dream, reality, past, present, future. Spun everywhere. Simon Relph, our producer, said there was no chance of anyone understanding this at all! So I wrote a second draft which was much more a psychological thriller — a police investigation, rather conventional and lame. Then I wrote a third draft that tried to combine the freewheelingness of the first with the narrative structure of the second.

Hare, interviewed by Steve Lawson, 'Hare Apparent',
Film Comment, Sept.-Oct. 1985, p. 19

As I sat in pubs and wine-bars in Yorkshire, men who stood around in grey flannels and green jackets and women who sat on bar-stools in two-piece suits seemed infinitely more mysterious than the exotic creatures I knew in London. I just knew that I wanted to write about the romance and mystery of small-town middle-class life and the film is meant to be about what it's like to live in England now for a lot of people. Most films about this background show the people as rather limited in their intelligence, desires, and imagination. What the film is claiming — which seems to me optimistic — is that people who are dismissed as bourgeois souls are as full of passion and feeling as opera-singers, but they happen, because they're English, to repress these feelings. You could accuse the film of being a romantic view of the world. But if you open your eyes to how people actually behave it's there. . . . I used to read a lot of thrillers. . . . Dick Francis was much in my mind in *Wetherby* because what he does is create a world which isn't real but which is truthful.

Hare, interviewed by Michael Billington,
'What Excites Me about *Pravda*', *The Guardian*, 2 Mar. 1985, p. 12

In any narrative in which dream plays a large part, film wins hands down. There is a strong prejudice still in the British film industry against screenwriters directing their own work. . . . Yet on a film as deeply felt as *Wetherby* I found I had almost no choice. The eye which first sees the

dream must also recreate it. . . . This is a Wetherby of my imagination.
> Hare, 'How to Spend a Million',
> *Sunday Times*, 3 Mar. 1985, p. 39

Wetherby is my privet-hedge film. It's about what it's like to be brought up in suburban respectability, in which any kind of emotional out-goingness is frowned upon.
> Hare, interviewed by Mel Gussow,
> 'David Hare: Playwright as Provocateur',
> *New York Times*, 29 Sept. 1985, p. 45

It's about a woman who for thirty years regretted something she did a long time ago and cannot speak about it. The English are a repressed people. The class system — if you're in the lower middle class — teaches you not to draw attention to yourself, not to do anything too obtrusive, not to put your head up above the parapet. And she feels that she's not entitled to make emotional demands on other people. Nobody ever writes about a middle-aged woman with a sexual need. . . . While she represses her feelings, he is an emotional junkie who'd do anything for a sensation. Psychopaths are supposed to be marked by an absence of feeling; but he's a psychopath who's desperate for feeling.
> Hare, interviewed by Dan Yakir, 'Hare Style',
> *Horizon*, Dec. 1985, p. 45

The social structure which Alan Bennett parodies in *A Private Function* is one of the reasons why *Wetherby* is set in Wetherby, for it is a locale in which Hare clearly suggests that the question of values might still be seriously posed. . . . *Wetherby* turns on the contrast of scale and setting, the cosiness of the town and its characters, the cosiness of English theatrical life, the family concern and the old boy network, with the grandeur of emotion and the magnitude of the issues individuals have to confront. How do you handle great moral questions if you are neither Shakespeare nor capable of being the voice of a nascent imperial power?
> Jill Forbes, 'The Long Arm of the Theatre',
> *Sight and Sound*, Spring 1985, p. 140-1

The film focuses on a certain middle-class strata, cast comfortably adrift in the Thatcher era with nowhere to go, and emotionally incapable even of spirited reaction. And what Hare lays out before us in his study of Yorkshire's well-heeled suburbia is not the applied cynicism of *The Ploughman's Lunch*, but the capacity for emotional upheaval just underneath the starched surface. . . . What Hare achieves, not without effort and in spite of an occasionally over-ambitious density, is a kind of political theatre that engages on an acutely personal level. None of these people, except possibly the suicide, can articulate what's happening to them. Nor, seemingly, would they wish to. The film's chief task is to do that for them, without being aggressively schematic.

Derek Malcolm, 'The Mourning after the Night Before',
The Guardian , 7 Mar. 1985

For a working model we need look no further than *The Cocktail Party*: in *Wetherby*, too, there is a Mysterious Stranger who will change everyone's life. . . . We discover that the Mysterious Stranger was marked by a 'central disfiguring blankness', and was obscurely motivated by anger or sexuality: in his death we might also be meant to see an emblem for the general mood of impoverishment and gloom which invades all of the other characters. Other meanings may be lurking here (one's suspicions are aroused by David Hare's professed inability to understand the real significance of the film), but a narrative which veers between a sad monotone and cryptic violence may quite possibly have forfeited the larger significance which comes from a more comprehensive vision. . . . It would not be pushing the theatrical analogy too far to describe the actors as actorish; to put it another way, the cast seems to exhibit that particular range of emotions which contemporary performers always seem to adopt and which will, in a generation or two, seem as remote and as unrealistic as the gestures of Duse or a Bernhardt: the wintry smiles, the painful attempts at communication, the defeated gestures, the sad honesty. . . . What *Wetherby* has to say about the state of contemporary Britain (which apparently is one of its aspects) is anybody's guess: the country, at least in its northern areas, is depicted as being at an extremely low ebb, both gloomy and inconsequential, and with a tendency to sporadic violence which only confirms the forebodings of every one concerned; most of these characters are invaded by hopelessness, or at least lack of ambition, and they suffer from a certain weary impoverishment of feeling.

Peter Ackroyd, 'Modern Times',
The Spectator, 16 Mar. 1985, p. 39-40

Pravda: a Fleet Street Comedy

A play in two acts, with Howard Brenton.

First production: Olivier Th., 2 May 1985 (dir. Hare;
   with Anthony Hopkins as Lambert Le Roux, Tim McInnerny as
   Andrew May, and Bill Nighy as Sylvester).
First U.S. production: Guthrie Th., Minneapolis, Jan. 1989.
Published: Methuen, 1985.

The play follows the fortunes of Andrew May, a reporter on the
Leicester Bystander, *and the South African media magnate and
sports promoter Lambert Le Roux, who buys the* Bystander *and
appoints Andrew as its editor. Le Roux then buys the* Daily Tide,
*'a ranting, nipple-ridden broadsheet' in London, and enlists the
help of an MP, Peter Quince, to acquire the* Daily Victory, *'the
only newspaper with England on its masthead'. He sacks the*
Victory's *editor and replaces him with Andrew. At the
beginning of Act Two Andrew wins an Editor of the Year award.
His wife Rebecca, daughter of the former owner of the*
Bystander, *comes in with a Ministry of Defence document about
a plutonium leak cover-up, which Andrew is about to publish
when Le Roux appears and sacks him. Andrew and Rebecca
sink the* Victory's *chief competitor, the* Usurper, *with the
repercussions of the nuclear story, and consequently join forces
with the previous editor, Quince, and Le Roux's personal
assistant, to outbid Le Roux for ownership of the* Usurper. *They
publish 'revelations' about Le Roux's personal life which prove
untrue, and Le Roux sues them for libel. The play ends at the*
Daily Tide, *which Le Roux amalgamates with the* Victory, *with
Andrew as editor. The* Victory *resembles* The Times *and the*
Daily Tide *the* Sun, *and some of the characters have probable
real-life models.*

It takes the state of Fleet Street as a metaphor for what is in the air
generally. The play says that if you were a visitor from Mars and came
here and read the *Mail*, the *Express*, the *Telegraph*, *The Times*, the
Sunday Times, and *Sunday Telegraph*, the *Sun* and most of the others
you would conclude that the relation of government to newspapers was
much as it was in the Soviet Union. Those of us who live here know that
to be untrue. So what the play is asking is what is it about Thatcherism
that is so appealing. . . . Howard and I are not bitching any particular
paper or person. We're trying to teach people to decode newspapers

because we think there's a great deal of news management and that what passes for news isn't.

Hare, interviewed by Michael Billington,
'What Excites Me about *Pravda*', *The Guardian*, 2 Mar. 1985, p. 12

The play could never be about being a journalist. That's been so much better done by Arnold Wesker. We're interested in power, the exercise and abuse of power and the really nasty things that people do to each other in the process of acquiring and holding on to power.

Hare, interviewed by Steve Grant, 'Act All about It',
The Observer, 28 Apr. 1985, p. 21

We both dreamt of the kind of play we enjoy seeing when we go to the theatre — big plays, full of characters and incident, comedies, taking on large subjects — and we willed one into existence. . . . Why are the papers so willing to get into bed with government? Or with this particular government? It's usually the proprietors who are blamed. We're not so sure. In Fleet Street, it's convenient for journalists to blame everything on proprietors. . . . We plan the plot very thoroughly indeed, by argument. Then hang the dialogue on at the last possible moment. The dialogue is the reward for all the hard work you do on the plot.

Hare and Brenton,
note in programme to National Theatre production, 1985

It is an illiterate strip-cartoon, cruder by far than the worst excesses of any newspaper possessed of photographs depicting a trouserless vicar in the company of the chief bellringer's wife. . . . Never yet did I read a newspaper story that was simultaneously as ignorant, erroneous, unchecked, ill-written, and reckless as *Pravda*.

Bernard Levin, 'The Truth about this Play'
The Times, 29 Oct. 1985

As in most radical-chic agitprop, the villain is omnipotent and everyone else is totally helpless. This puts a severe strain on the rest of the cast, who try to compensate for their watery parts in any number of ways: they caper, huff and puff, sneer a lot, run about, mug and grimace, pose furiously, roll on the floor, frown severely, and climb on to furniture and wave their arms. Most of all — apparently with the director's encouragement — they shout. Time and again Hare ranges his actors in a row facing the audience and makes them bellow at the stalls. Alas, for all the gymnastics and noise, the good guys (and bad guys too, except for Hopkins's tycoon) remain a dull pack of posturing ninnies. The plot-line, barren of conflict and therefore of drama, is devoid of interest. Theatrical moments, when they occur (not often), spring from incidental sketches like Lambert Le Roux (Hopkins) playing at martial arts in his Japanese garden and costume. Some humour comes out of remarks — mostly by Le Roux — which score off the ninnies.

Herb Greer, 'Pravda',
Encounter, Sept.-Oct. 1985, p. 36-8

Pravda goes in for comic overkill, stringing together as many jokes as it can in order to make sure that some hit its target, churning out endless examples of Fleet Street duplicity and presenting them as buffoonery. The trouble is that because the target seems so obvious, the play does not know what its target is. Is it the triviality of the tabloids or the stuffiness of the 'serious' press, drunken drama critics or psychotic editors, provincial hacks or international tycoons? . . . At times it seems, like Private Eye, an extension of the malaise it lampoons. . . . What starts out as a leftist spoofing of Thatcherism ends up as a patriotic ode to bumbling incompetence. All press, young and old, left and right, cynics and idealists, end up at a dogtrack in Lancashire, all hoodwinked and all British, flying the flag at half mast because they have all been well and truly screwed.

The way is open for the Super villain to dominate the stage and Anthony Hopkins does not need any second chance. He struts around like a cross between a bull and a ballerina, his thick torso stuck archly forward, yet tripping lightly on his toes. As others speak, he appears neither to notice nor listen, but lets his weasel's eyes scan the audience with open menace. It is a ritual of unashamed hypnosis. We watch Hopkins and cease to listen to others. We grow impatient for his next entrance. The true test here for Hare and Brenton is whether they can feed the monster they have created with dialogue equal to his evil magnificence. The answer is — only in fits and starts. He has to bluff his way through silly scenes where he practises martial arts at home in Weybridge, brings royalty down into the press offices, and then fires half his staff in public. The authors' Frankenstein is too large for the farce they create, too sinister in his powers of easy manipulation to be hidebound by a trivial and clichéd plot. . . .

There is a limit, too, to the suspension of disbelief. The open V-shaped stage gives us an elaborate open plan press office where the teaboy can hear all. The office is done in lavish and precise naturalistic detail, but many of the conversations which take place there are pure fantasy.

John Orr, 'A Knave and Too Many Fools',
Literary Review, June 1985, p. 19-20

More black farce than comedy, it is funny in a Punch and Judy knockabout way, full of clichés in character and dialogue (the lone ineffectual voice for truth, Andrew's wife, is a university graduate in investigative journalism, peace-activist, ILEA-teacher) with real-life parallels plain to see. Parts of its construction would shame a novice (the newsvendors' chorus; the chance encounter on the Yorkshire Moors) as would its parade of stage types (footling bishop, 'castle creeper' trade unionist, drunken drama critic, etc.) which provide good actors with excellent opportunities for caricature.

John James, 'News Revue',
Times Educational Supplement, 10 May 1985

Le Roux appears a positive dynamo, decisive and potent. He emerges as one of the most attractive stage villains since Richard III. . . . I can't see the comedy in this. It smacks of political capitulation. . . . This is not the 'first time modern Fleet Street has been put on the stage'. Wesker did it with *The Journalists*, an altogether more optimistic play. Between the two plays Wesker's view of the journalist as a positive agent fighting to reveal the truth has degenerated into Brenton and Hare's view of the journalist as a spineless, professional toady, easily bought, exploited and sold by the forces of political repression. That is not funny.

Clive Barker, *British Book News*, Sept. 1985, p. 561

Le Roux has a life of his own, and on the grand scale. In Anthony Hopkins's brilliant, buoyant realization, he is portrayed as a comic creation as monstrously beguiling as Tartuffe. He shares with Molière's sham holy man the gift of ever renewed plausibility. . . . *Pravda* is not merely lamenting the newspapers that are but pining for newspapers that might be. . . . It recalls the morally assertive best of warmhearted Broadway satires like *The Solid Gold Cadillac* in every regard save one: *Pravda* does not and, given its bitter conviction, could not have a happy ending.

William A. Henry III, 'Savaging the "Foundry of Lies" ',
Time, 10 June 1985

No one could say that the authors of *Pravda* set out to flatter the prejudices of anyone, such as myself, professionally engaged in Fleet Street. By my count our trade is convicted of the following vices: ambition, cruelty, cynicism, incompetence, complacency, defeatism, snobbery, bias, deception, plagiarism, triviality, sycophancy (to politicians as well as to owners), cowardice, corruption, of being opinionated, arrogant, and drunk, of lacking convictions, of having fantasies about our own power and influence, and no solidarity. To set against this catalogue of sins, what virtues can we offer? The authors allow us hardly any — a sentimental attachment to the rituals of the game (the noise of the presses, the bustle of deadlines, that sort of thing), just a faint spark of rebellious idealism in one character, perhaps, which is soon snuffed or charmed out of him. Then there's Rebecca, the so-called 'graduate in investigative journalism' and the chosen voice of conscience in the play: what is *her* solution? All she can suggest to her editor-husband is that he should assert his integrity by getting out of 'this filthy profession'. . . . *Pravda* holds up a mirror to Fleet Street all right — and if the image seems distorted in some ways, we have only ourselves to blame. But the mirror *does* distort, none the less. . . . My main reservation about the play is not that it is rude to journalists, but that it places too much weight on the supposed malign influence of proprietors as the source of all our ills.

Donald Trelford, 'Fleet Street through the Looking-Glass',
The Observer, 12 May 1985, p. 8

See also:

Howard Brenton, 'Writing for Democratic Laughter', *Drama*, No. 3, 1985, p. 9-11.

The Bay at Nice

A one-act play.
First production: Cottesloe Th., 9 Sept. 1986, in a double-bill with
   Wrecked Eggs (dir. Hare; with Irene Worth as Valentina).
Published: with *Wrecked Eggs*, Faber, 1986.

The heroine (superbly played by Irene Worth with just a hint of a foreign accent) is, as a former student of Matisse in Paris during the Belle Epoque, a repository of recent western history. Elegant and contemptuous of Soviet austerities, Valentina has been invited to an unnamed museum, presumably the Hermitage, by a young polyester-suited card-carrying and careerist assistant curator (Colin Stinton) to authenticate the painting of Hare's title as a genuine Matisse. Like all of Hare's plays — or indeed, any work which questions moral standards — this is basically a piece about authenticity: what constitutes a true work of art? love? decent work? a valid life? . . . Sophia (Zoë Wanamaker), Valentina's homely and plodding daughter (conceived in one of those Parisian moments of 'lying around in beds with men in studios' and a thorn in the formerly unfettered flesh ever since), arrives in the hope of enlisting her mother's help in her divorce from her 'model husband of the State'. She introduces Valentina to her new lover (Philip Locke), a tall, gentle, aged, and improbable suitor who toils on the outskirts of upward mobility for the sanitation department. After many savage utterances on Sophia's person, her amateur and merely 'photographic' painting, her lack of ambition and misapprehensions of love, Valentina most implausibly offers to sell her own flat to pay for her daughter's divorce. Then, alone, she removes the drapes from the painting and, from her expression and her series of happy feints round it (almost a matador's with a bull), we know the picture to be the real thing: a relic, we suppose, of an age of idealism, when personal definitions of freedom and discipline weren't state-controlled.

Victoria Radin, 'Put Asunder',
New Statesman, 26 Sept. 1986, p. 30-1

The debate, although it resists schematic analysis, seems to favour the uncompromising mother; an unfashionable resolution. Certainly Irene Worth, with her haughty disdain for cant and moral fudge, succeeds in earning our respect. Here is a fine classical actress creating a character of severe moral grandeur through whom Hare can challenge a prevailing idea of 'freedom'.

Christopher Edwards, 'Moral Imperatives',
The Spectator, 27 Sept. 1986, p. 47

The history of Russia in the twentieth century is alluded to in *The Bay at Nice*. The characters speak of the emigration to Paris in the 1920s, of the Party and of socialist realism. These questions are not obtrusively dwelt upon, however; Hare's concerns transcend his context, and his eloquence and wit provide an absorbing variation.

Julian Graffy, 'Culture and Consumption',
Times Literary Supplement, 26 Sept. 1986, p. 1064

I think that consciously Hare is on the side of the weak and the living; but there's a frosty sub-text to the play which glorifies the remote and the strong; and I shall never forget Irene Worth as she finally gazes at the painting, her face bathed in a halo of proud, lonely, superhuman transfiguration.

John Peter, 'A Portrait of Fatal Power',
Sunday Times, 14 Sept. 1986, p. 51

The play's force is diminished because Valentina's crucial contradiction is incompletely written. But this remains a mouth-wateringly dense affair, enlivened by Wildean touches. 'I act as if I'm rich', pronounces the impoverished matriarch. 'It seems to me simply good manners.'

Jim Hiley, 'Hostile Climates', *The Listener*, 18 Sept. 1986, p. 32

See also reviews of the double-bill, p. 71, below.

Wrecked Eggs

A one-act play.
First production: Cottesloe Th., 9 Sept. 1986, in a double-bill with *The Bay at Nice* (dir. Hare).
Published: with *The Bay at Nice*, Faber, 1986.

A youngish couple (Colin Stinton and Kate Buffery), on the point of separation, rap on with a party guest (Zoë Wanamaker) who has just had an abortion, and not for the first time either. . . . The atmosphere is relaxed and sensuous. There's masses of food. There's a pool, and a beach nearby. The body is all-important: its well-being tells you who you are. For Robbie, the husband, a relationship is like real estate: he has invested in it, so it must flourish. There's a sad and brittle sterility about this couple as they prepare to part.

John Peter, 'A Portrait of Fatal Power',
Sunday Times, 14 Sept. 1986, p. 51

[Hare is] in no hurry to get to the point but is off up a succession of by-ways, very few of which lead even circuitously back to the main road, and the impression is of ambling along genially to nowhere in particular. It is not unamusing. The superficial small-talk produces a crop of flip epigrams which, God knows, are not to be despised: if you had this sort of chatter at your dinner-table twice or thrice a year you'd be lucky. Those would be the occasions when the hand-picked guests come along with all their lines rehearsed, just hoping to steer the conversation into the right cues. That's much the ways things are in *Wrecked Eggs*, except that all the voices are Hare's and he has vagrant thoughts considerably to do with sex, including the effectiveness of Diet Coke as a spermicide, Grace being an incessantly fertile girl who has done a lot of practical research along these lines. But we also get to such topics as the ethics of espionage (Robbie has changed his name in an effort to live down his father's conviction for spying) and room is found for a few pot-shots at the press which maybe couldn't be fitted into *Pravda*.

Kenneth Hurren, *Plays and Players*,
Nov. 1986, p. 21

Wrecked Eggs is the more appealing, being witty about contemporary society, which Hare knows, in a manner clearly impossible when writing about Leningrad in the 1950s. Hare also seems to want to be more restrained in his satire of Stalinist Russia, but is prepared to let himself go in his attacks on the United States, and malice is usually more entertaining. . . . This could be John Updike territory — but there isn't a feeling of pain. This could be Woody Allen, but it isn't funny enough. It doesn't reveal Hare at his best, for his mind is too resolutely set against U.S. opulence and casual cruelty.

John Elsom, *Plays International*, Oct. 1986, p. 24-5

Hare has a cool, sardonic eye for modern manners and he pins down beautifully the absurdities of New York life: the workaholic lawyer's belief that pleasure is an extra and that quality of life is a commodity to be purchased, along with the assumption that marital separation is a 'rite of passage' to be marked by a party. . . . What makes *Wrecked Eggs* a better play [than *The Bay at Nice*] is that it clearly springs from direct observation and that, through the character of the press agent, it focuses on real moral dilemmas: how to hold on to a belief in right and wrong in a materialistic world, whether to opt for the dignity of solitude or the pleasures of commitment. Zoë Wanamaker is spot-on as the press agent: she suggests the practised observer of other people's crack-ups and yet someone with burning troubles of her own. Colin Stinton hints precisely at the perennial boyishness of many American males.

Michael Billington, *The Guardian*, 10 Sept. 1986

The Bay at Nice and *Wrecked Eggs*

Taken together the plays represent interesting essays in a genre — the play of ideas — that English playwrights do not usually handle well at all. Both examine the conflicting demands of personal fulfilment and responsibility; themes that confirm Hare to be a moralist.

Christopher Edwards, 'Moral Imperatives',
The Spectator, 27 Sept. 1986, p. 48

Parallels and contrasts between the two plays soon become apparent. In the first a couple are attempting to come together, in the second about to part. In each a third character, a woman, questions the rightness not just of this action, but of all the couple's assumptions. . . . Hare writes about Europeans and Americans, about deprivation and excess, culture and consumption. For a European audience it is unsurprising, perhaps even initially flattering to find his Americans trite and vulgar, his Europeans intense and complex, but, to quote Hare, 'Is it right?' One cannot help noticing that the dice are loaded. The main Russian protagonists are an artist and her teacher daughter; the American couple a lawyer and his tennis coach wife. The Russian sanitation engineer responds with radiant joy to talk of Matisse. Would Hare let his American equivalent do likewise? Does he believe that European sanitation engineers are more cultured? Is he right?

Julian Graffy, 'Culture and Consumption',
Times Literary Supplement, 26 Sept. 1986, p. 1064

In some ways both plays are variations on the theme of pain and departure first touched on by Hare in his fine television film *Dreams of Leaving*. Even Valentina has to wrench herself from the memory of Matisse's tutelage, and the catalytic presence of the press agent extends the marital agony for a few more days. All the time the characters are asked to confront the present at the expense of the past. Valentina admires — chilling speech, this — Matisse's inability to remember his children's names. The work came first. Happiness too, and how we estimate it, looms in both plays. The Russian wife has no money and is unhappy, the New York couple too much of it and are still miserable.

Michael Coveney, *Financial Times*, 10 Sept. 1986

The Knife

Musical, with lyrics by Tim Rose Price and music by Nick Bicât.

The Knife

First production: by New York Shakespeare Festival at Public/Newman Th., 12 Feb. 1987 (dir. Hare; with Mandy Patinkin as Peter). *Unpublished.*

The story of Peter, a married transsexual with three kids, coming to terms with his new female identity. . . . Despite his lovely wife, Angela, and delightful children, Peter, the pre-eminently manly, prosperous-seeming chef in a hotel restaurant, suffers from vague unease. One night, Jenny, an airline hostess with a propensity for brutal lovers ('Why does love have to end with a slap in the face?'), escapes from one of them to a hotel room and orders a late-night sandwich. Peter, the only person left in the kitchen, brings her one, and is received by her in the nude. He hands her a robe, and she exclaims, 'From the way you look at me, you could be a woman.' Suddenly, a light goes on in his mind: he needs a sex-change operation. If this doesn't satisfy your craving for the absurd, never fear: there is plenty more where that came from. Jenny falls in love with Peter, who refuses to wait out the two years prescribed by the National Health and cannot afford the £10,000 for a private operation — oh, yes, despite everyone's solidly American accent, we are in England. So Jenny pays for it, even accompanies Peter abroad for the surgery, and is repaid by his telling her it is all her vengeance on men, as he sends her packing.

> John Simon, 'Victor Victorious',
> *New York*, 23 Mar. 1987, p. 89-90

[Hare] substitute[s] intellectualizing for thought, murkiness of characterization for the mysteries of behaviour. How can a musical dramatize a man's choice of sexual identity if its creators can't bring themselves to make such mundane choices as the identity of his profession and the location of his home? In lieu of the specific details that might illuminate Peter and draw us into his rending predicament, the writers indulge in remote, highfalutin metaphors. . . . When the libretto does eschew its fuzzy abstractions for concrete drama, it either embraces clichés or strains credulity. . . . Such is the smug, right-minded tone of *The Knife* that its few instances of originality — notably paired, comic songs contrasting homosexual and heterosexual chauvinism — come off flatter than they might in a friskier context. Mr. Hare . . . harms his cause this time by staging a large-cast musical as if it were a three-character play with extras. . . . Bicât's accomplished score — which falters only when it panders to conventional pop and Broadway tastes — is expertly served as well by the strings and woodwinds of Chris Walker's lush orchestrations.

Frank Rich, *New York Times*, 11 Mar. 1987, Sec. C, p. 22

Essentially, Mr. Hare (as author and director) and his collaborators . . . are taking no position — moral, medical or sexual — but are letting theatregoers make up their own minds about the need for the drastic surgery. . . . In his other plays, Mr. Hare has often maintained a position of cool objectivity — but with far greater emotional complexity. . . . The difference is that Susan Traherne, Victor Mehta, and Lambert Le Roux are fully realized dramatic creations. . . . Peter-Liz, however, remains an enigma. One assumes that *The Knife* was created with the most earnest intentions (and the earnestness repeatedly blocks the author's natural theatricality). The purpose, it would seem — in keeping with themes in Mr. Hare's other work — is an investigation of mendacity and of role-playing as a way of life. . . . Peter-Liz is a self-made outcast. In the turning point of *The Knife*, an elegantly dressed surgeon flicks his scalpel as a switchblade, and, with a smile, sings about the operation to come. It is unclear if the scene is meant to be serious, satiric, or savage. . . . As an operatic equivalent of a problem play, *The Knife* is problematic, and a sidestep in Mr. Hare's theatrical career.

Mel Gussow, 'What Pushes David Hare's Characters', *New York Times*, 15 Mar. 1987, Sec. II, p. 5

The Secret Rapture

A two-act play.
First production: Lyttelton Th., 4 Oct. 1988 (dir. Howard Davies; with Penelope Wilton as Marion and Jill Baker as Isobel).
First U.S. production: Public Th., 1989 (previews); Barrymore Th., 26 Oct. 1989 (dir. Hare; with Blair Brown as Marion).
Published: Faber, 1988.

The Secret Rapture *is a play for today. Robert's death leaves his daughters, thrusting Tory Junior Environment Minister Marion and humane commercial artist Isobel, to look after their irresponsible stepmother Kath. Kath is everything Marion loathes: loose, boozy, feckless, lazy, blackmailing others with her careless helplessness. Patient, long-suffering, caring Isobel (whose qualities are turned against her by Marion's and Kath's unfounded accusations of judgmental self-righteousness) takes her on, losing her livelihood, her lover and her life thereby. Isobel's integrity is proof against the me-firstism of everyone else in the play. Her goodness exposes their selfishness to hilarious and tragic effect. Act One's satirical exposure of contemporary political mores and business ethics is bitingly funny. Like Hare we are fascinated and appalled by Marion's outspoken ruthlessness, her dedication to power, money, success. Act Two shifts gear to a deeper level. Hare's searing insight into male/female relationships of dependency and need, his revelation of Marion's inner insecurity, the suggestion that Isobel's death is redemptive, are profoundly serious and moving.*

John James, 'Personal Relations',
Times Educational Supplement, 14 Oct. 1988, p. 28

What is The Secret Rapture?

It's that moment at which a nun expects to be united with Christ. In other words, it's death.

How did you get the idea for the play?

From my closeness to a friend whose father had recently died, I should say in circumstances entirely different from those in the play . . . .

I'm interested in how to write about the 'eighties. What's noticeable so far about the most popular plays of this decade is that they borrow their vitality from immoral characters. The audience gets its kick from just how fast the handcart's going to hell. One of my favourite recent plays is *Aunt Dan and Lemon*, in which the two leading characters are neo-fascists. You only have to think of the real estate men in *Glengarry Glen Ross*, or the dealers in *Serious Money*, or, for that matter, of Lambert Le Roux in *Pravda*, to see that modern plays have seemed, perhaps unintentionally, to end up celebrating malign energy. Or at least they hitch a ride from their villains. Look at *Les Liaisons Dangereuses*. I'm trying in this play perhaps to buck the trend. Unfashionably, I have a heroine.

Hare, interviewed by Anne Busby,
programme of National Theatre production, 1988

In Catholic theology, the 'secret rapture' is the moment when the nun will become the bride of Christ: so it means death, or love of death, or death under life.

Hare, 'Love, Death and Edwina',
The Listener, 15 Sept. 1988, p. 38

It's either the Great Play or a load of old tosh. I think it is a very unusual play for the moment. There has been an awful lot about the economic consequences of Thatcherism in England and there's been brilliant work — in particular *The Boys from the Blackstuff* [by Alan Bleasdale, for television] — about the effect of Thatcherism on people's lives. But there's been very little about the psychology of Thatcherism. For some reason, she's generated very little fiction and there's been no real studies of the mentality of the people around her and what they want. It is an unfashionable play in that it is a tragedy. We don't have many plays with heroines or many tragedies in England at the moment. It is commonly said that it's not possible to write a tragedy nowadays and I was interested to see whether it was.

Hare, interviewed by Robert Crew,
'Playwright Hare Feels the Sting of Controversy',
Toronto Star, 11 Feb. 1989, Sec. F, p. 3

The only trouble is: what is it *about*? Needless to say, if you don't buy the whole business of the playwright as thinker, you probably won't care whether you know precisely what the thought behind David Hare's new play *The Secret Rapture* is. . . . I do not pretend to know just what Hare is getting at on a philosophical level, and for most of the way I do not mind very much. It is only when, in the second half, the play begins to fall into disconnected set pieces, sexy, melodramatic, or Chekhovian dying-fall, as though Hare himself does not know where he is going and is casting round desperately for some way to tie it all up, that I begin to get restive and look for the thread of Thought which might explain, in the author's mind if never quite on stage, what he can possibly be doing. . . . Some are certain that Isobel is a saint, a wholly good woman beleaguered by a naughty world. But she would seem to lack the ruthlessness of the real saint. Most of what she does she does from cowardice and the inability to resist.

John Russell Taylor, *Plays International*, Nov. 1988, p. 23-4

This demanding, sharp, and occasionally very funny play, crisply performed by a skilful cast, poses more questions than it answers. Is it political satire? Probably not, though politicians are satirized roundly and it pokes about at the issues in contemporary debate. Is it a comedy of contemporary manners? Yes and no: full, frequent, and enthusiastic enunciation of 'fuck' speaks for yes, but the absence of any cheap stereotypes beyond politicians and graphic designers — creatures of the 1960s and 1970s, surely — suggests no. Is it timeless tragedy? Up to a point, but nothing is absolutely timeless which can nail the deformed personality of a female Conservative minister so convincingly to the floor. . . . As a playwright Hare seems to find it difficult to resist the temptation to set intellectual puzzles. If this play seems to be an uneasy hybrid of Ibsen and *Serious Money*, he must bear some of the responsibility.

> John Turner, 'Dramas of Domination',
> *Times Literary Supplement*, 14 Oct. 1988, p. 1148

What few people noticed first time round — myself included — was that this is a deeply optimistic play which says that the English virtues of tolerance, consideration and humanity will in the last resort triumph over the historical aberration of Thatcherism. It is difficult to prove this without giving everything away; but the final image of the play unequivocally shows that the Isobels of this world will win out over the Marions and that harmony and peace will return to our diseased, temporarily unrecognizable Britain.

> Michael Billington, 'Year of Smooth Transition',
> *Plays International*, Dec. 1988-Jan. 1989, p. 25

Clothes seem to be all important in expressing, almost in cartoon terms, the attributes of the characters. Penelope Wilton as Marion wears the sort of smart Windsmoor type suits favoured by Tory women MPs, while her predatory assistant, Rhonda, goes in for sex-and-power dressing with big shoulders and short skirts. Katherine flaunts herself in strapless taffeta, and Isobel dons a voluminous white raincoat halfway through the play, giving the impression of sexless otherworldliness as she approaches her martyrdom.

> Clare Colvin, *Plays and Players*, Nov.-Dec. 1988, p. 17-18

[Hare] seems uniquely prepared to write of the human cost of current British policies. Among his major contemporaries, Alan Ayckbourn does indeed write about the darker realities of modern family life in Britain, and Caryl Churchill in *Serious Money* writes of the corruption of the City; but Hare alone relates public to private morality.

> Sheridan Morley, 'Hare's Breadth', *Punch*, 28 Oct. 1988, p. 65

Hare's painful, witty, and moving new play *The Secret Rapture* is a morality of modern behaviour in which the people who have all the answers face, buy out, and destroy the people who thought there were no questions to ask. The elements are traditional but neglected: a representative of earthly government, an artist, an artisan, a man of God, a witch. Hare also brings off a portrait of absolute goodness on stage, while a conflict between sisters transforms a fatal attraction into a *crime passionnel*, rare in any English play. . . . When read, the play's resonance seems political and its tensions absolutely sharp. In Howard Davies's production they are more elusive. John Gunter's handsome designs — oak panelling, office walls, bare floor, and great tree — provide a stark, reductive setting for these English lives rather than the clutter they sometimes suggest.

Michael Ratcliffe, *The Observer*, 9 Oct. 1988, p. 43

Hare has written one of the best English plays since the war and established himself as the finest British dramatist of his generation. *The Secret Rapture* is a family play; it is also the first major play to judge the England of the 1980s in terms that are both human and humane. . . . This is an uncomfortable play, full of a moving, brooding humanity and a hard, unforgiving sense of justice. It is a deeply marxist play too: not in a slick, flimsy party-political sense, but in a grand humanist sense which unites Marx with English radical and social thinkers such as Godwin. Hare is arguing that our values are shaped by the world we live in, just as we in turn shape that world in our own image. Both aggression and consent carry a responsibility. If you regard people as merely assets, then asset-stripping is the greatest sin: both presumption and murder. . . . The acting has a hard, compassionate luminosity, like strong but distant lights in a dark night. There's no spare gesture, no superfluous feeling.

John Peter, 'Moral Masterpiece for our Times',
Sunday Times, 9 Oct. 1988, Sec. C, p. 8

Paris by Night

Film.
Released: 1989 (dir. Hare; with Charlotte Rampling as Clara,
   Michael Gambon as Gerald, Robert Hardy as Adam Gillvray, and
   Jane Asher as Pauline).
Published: Faber, 1988.

It is a thriller, a murder story, and the sole purpose is to scare the hell out of people.

Hare, interviewed by Carol Lawson, 'At the Movies',
New York Times, 11 Oct. 1985

Although there has been a considerable body of films and plays about the economic results of Thatcherism, there has been almost nothing of consequence about the characteristics and personalities of those who have ruled over us during these last eight years. It is one of the greatest mysteries of Thatcherism that it has generated so little fiction.

Hare, 'Introduction', *Paris by Night*, p. vii

The key ingredients in Hare's latest stage play, *The Secret Rapture*, recur — a female Thatcherite politician with a weak husband, financial chicanery visited upon the innocent by unscrupulous entrepreneurs, a woman shot five times at point-blank range by a desperate man, a wimpish young hero speaking on behalf of decency in a voice that would register dead on a heart-monitoring machine. But whereas the play is enacted wholly in the domestic arena, the movie (like Hare's *Plenty*) moves uneasily on to the public scene and takes the form of a *film noir* thriller. . . . [Clara Paige, the Tory MP] has a past tainted by cheating a business partner and driving him into bankruptcy, and a corrupt present symbolized by the alcoholic MP husband and the neglected eight-year-old son she has sacrificed to her career. An anonymous phone-caller issues disturbing threats, the Ibsenesque ex-business associate makes veiled blackmail demands, an agreeable menacing mood is established. Then Clara is sent to represent HMG at some rather vague trade negotiations in Paris (the knowing tone fails to conceal Hare's ignorance of, and indifference towards, political processes), where she meets a tedious young prig who opens her eyes to a supposedly richer life (honest, warm, familial, Jewish). Wandering in a romantic daze back to her hotel through the Parisian night, she sees the English blackmailer alone on a bridge, an encounter so unlikely that one initially supposes it to be an hallucination. But it's for real, and in a split-second she's tipped the hapless fellow into the river, hoping presumably that at worst she'll cop a plea of 'guilty but in Seine.' . . . It is indeed Hare's point that Tories preach morality while being allowed to get away with anything from adultery to murder.

Philip French, 'Hare and the Tortoise',
The Observer, 4 June 1989, p. 44

The political morality tale is weakened by the demands of a thriller melodrama. Hare is a very promising film-maker, and at first the film builds up the drama and the characters swiftly and elliptically. In the later stages, however, the development becomes laborious and contrived, and the characters lose their conviction. . . . Charlotte Rampling admirably juxtaposes the character's public confidence and private fears; Michael Gambon, with ponderous movements and a face drained of expression, makes the husband a surprisingly touching figure.

David Robinson, 'Right Dishonourable',
The Times, 1 June 1989, p. 18

The point, however, is not the lecture, but the mystery, and at the heart of the mystery is the powerful and powerfully alluring figure of Clara Paige, the sort of rangy, bad woman whom in another age Barbara Stanwyck might have been drawn to play. . . . The plot coasts along with tidy professionalism and an absence of loose ends. . . . The film gleams in the best burnished contemporary British manner.

John Pym, 'Mother England',
Sight and Sound, Spring 1989, p. 134

Paris by Night, an ideological thriller written and directed by David Hare, is disappointingly stagey. Under the close, naturalistic scrutiny of a movie camera, scenes that might conceivably work with live actors look flimsy or implausible. Charlotte Rampling is by far the best thing in Hare's mix of *film noir* and political tract, her aloof sensuality making Clara Paige a splendidly ambiguous 'forties-style heroine. But she always seems bemused by the creaky, melodramatic plot. . . . By subordinating his story to polemic, he weakens both. Popular genres can be very effectively used to make political points, but it takes a light touch and perhaps an instinct for allusiveness. Here, good intentions are sabotaged by Hare's need to preach.

Margaret Walters, 'Clara's Heartless',
The Listener, 8 June 1989, p. 34

Strapless

Film.
Released: 1989 (dir. Hare; with Blair Brown, Bruno Ganz, and
Bridget Fonda).

An American doctor working in an English NHS hospital meets a mysterious foreigner who falls in love with her and showers her with presents. Although knowing little of him, she decides to take the risk, and marries him. Soon afterwards he disappears, and she has to pay off his debts. Her sister, an easygoing dress-designer, is single and pregnant. The doctor discovers her husband is already married, and has devoted his life to romance, being unsuited to the everyday. She is inspired to take the lead in protesting against hospital cutbacks, while her sister proves to be a good mother. She is last seen in a strapless dress — which shouldn't stay up, but it does.

b: Translation

The Rules of the Game

English version, with Robert Rietty, of the play by Luigi Pirandello.
First London production: National Th. at New Th., 15 June 1971
  (dir. Anthony Page).

It was a shameful piece of work — the only thing I've ever done which wasn't absolutely what I believed in. I did it to make some money in order to do later what I wanted to do. But that never works. It's a play that I had some ideas about, but I failed to communicate them to the company or the director. So it was an unmitigated disaster from my point of view.

Hare, 'From Portable Theatre to Joint Stock',
Theatre Quarterly, No. 20, Dec. 1975-Feb. 1976, p. 111

Most 'educated' people think that we live in a decadent system. But if you're a writer, I think you have to follow it through; and it seems to me to be simply fiddling to write about anything else.

Interview with Hugh Hebert, 'Putting the Knuckle in',
The Guardian, 4 Mar. 1974

Playwriting is a ruthlessly truthful medium, and I've come to believe in it much more as I've gone on working. I think that the judgements the audience make show up insincerity, reveal the superficial, and more and more I have trouble writing until I've worked out in the greatest possible detail what I think myself about some subject or other, whatever I'm writing about.

'From Portable Theatre to Joint Stock', *Theatre Quarterly*,
No. 20, Dec. 1975-Feb. 1976, p. 111-12

I believe in what used to be called socialist realism, that you should try to show how things are and how things could be. Plays have tension if you do both; if you only show how things are it's boring and if you only show how they could be, it's strident and hollow. . . . My plays argue that the main reform needed is moral; at present people know that they are damaging themselves by their behaviour, and need to change. . . . There are people in my plays who think sexual reform is the key to the new society. I myself have doubts about that. . . . I try to make all my plays different, so that nobody can say they know what a David Hare play is going to be like. This is because of my dislike of the self-indulgent, self-pitying writer, always writing about his own problems. I deliberately avoid writing about myself, my world, and my experiences.

Interview with Oleg Kerensky, *The New British Drama*
(London, 1977), p. 185

One of the reasons for the theatre's possible authority, and for its recent general drift towards politics, is its unique suitability to displaying an age in which men's ideals and men's practice bear no relation to each other; in which the public profession of, for example, socialism has often been reduced by the passage of history to wearying personal fetish, or even chronic personality disorder. The theatre is the best way of showing the gap between what is said and what is seen to be done. . . . The first question a political playwright addresses himself to is: why is it that in advanced industrial societies the record of revolutionary activity is so very miserable, so very, very low? . . . If a play is to be a weapon in the class struggle, then that weapon is not going to be the things you are saying; it is the interaction of what you are saying and what the audience is thinking. . . . For five years I have been writing history plays. I try to show the English their history. I write tribal pieces, trying to show how people behaved on this island, off this continental shelf, in this century. How this Empire vanished, how these ideals died. . . . We are living through a great, groaning, yawling festival of change — but because this is England it is not always seen on the streets. In my view it is seen in the extraordinary intensity of peoples' personal despair, and it is to that despair that as a historical writer I choose to address myself time and time again: in *Teeth 'n' Smiles*, in *Knuckle*, in *Plenty*. . . . I became a writer by default, to fill in the gaps, to work on areas of the fresco which were simply ignored, or appropriated for the shallowest purposes: rock music, black propaganda, gun-selling, diplomacy. . . . I write love stories. Most of my plays are that. Over and over again I have written about romantic love, because it never goes away.

'A Lecture Given at King's College, Cambridge, March 5, 1978',
Licking Hitler (Faber, 1978), p. 60-9

I don't like television drama, I don't like the look of it, the way it's produced; I don't like the censorship within the medium; I don't like the absurd circumstances under which the work has to be produced.

'After *Fanshen*: a Discussion',
in *Performance and Politics in Popular Drama*,
ed. David Bradby *et al.* (Cambridge, 1980), p. 307

I don't like to simplify my characters. What I try to do is not make people unrealistically morally right. I don't draw simple characters. . . . In all my plays, I've written that to do good is very hard; to do good looks evil, but it isn't like that at all. My plays are based on the idea that to live morally is a choice. . . . I tend to argue against my own good characters, possibly because I'm embarrassed since they often represent things that I represent. But what I'm saying is that given the present state of society, it is very difficult to live a moral life. . . . A play is what happens between the stage and the audience. What I've been trying to do in my later plays is to present them in such a way that the audience learn something abut their own values. . . . That's what I hope from my plays

— that they will incite people to have the courage of their own convictions. . . . There is a jealousy in my plays for those characters who see the outside world as enough. . . . I believe that there is no justice. You still see people going about the streets poor and Thatcher is still in power. . . . What I am sure about is that my love and my sympathy lies with those who seek justice however ludicrously they do so.

Interview with Judy Dempsey, *Literary Review*, 22 Aug. 1980, p. 35-6

Women are characteristically the conscience of my plays. They often stand one step outside a man's world, and so can see it much more clearly than those who are talking economics, all those things, through the way people relate to each other. . . . The boldest and most passionate statements of the theatre are things you've discovered and mean everything to you. And then you move on.

Interview with Benedict Nightingale,
'An Angry Young Man of the Eighties',
New York Times, 17 Oct. 1982, Sec. II, p. 6

I only ever thought of myself as a political playwright in the sense of trying to drag adult concerns into the theatre. I didn't see people psychologically and I didn't think people existed in their heads or in rooms; you had to put people into some sort of context. A lot of people's unhappiness would be explained by the time they lived in.

Interview with Carol Homden, 'A Dramatist of Surprise',
Plays and Players, Sept. 1988, p. 6

Nobody seems to have spotted it, but I've found myself in *Wetherby*, in *Paris by Night*, in *The Secret Rapture*, and in *Strapless* drawn more and more to feeling that there's something which isn't just what we're conditioned by. . . . If a writer doesn't have a sense of the other, by which I mean spirit or soul, I don't want to know.

Interview with Vera Lustig, 'Soul Searching',
Drama, No. 4, 1988, p. 18

I have a facility for dialogue, but it's gradually becoming sparer and less flashy because the dialogue was taking over the plays. Film writing has been very good for me, because the images allow you to create very profound feeling with few words. A self-consciousness about dialogue is a weakness of mine I've tried to do something about.

Interview with John Dugdale, 'Love, Death and Edwina',
The Listener, 15 Sept. 1988, p. 39

sidebar: 4: A Select Bibliography

a: Primary Sources

Collections of Plays

The Asian Plays (Faber, 1986) contains *Fanshen*, *Saigon*, and
 A Map of the World.
The History Plays (Faber, 1984) contains *Knuckle*,
 Licking Hitler, and *Plenty*.

*All Hare's other plays are separately published: see under
individual titles in Section 2 for bibliographical details.*

Articles and Essays

Reviews of crime novels, *The Spectator*, 1970.
'A Lecture Given at King's College, Cambridge', *Licking
 Hitler* (Faber, 1978), p. 57-71.
'Time of Unease', *At the Royal Court*, ed. Richard Findlater
 (Ambergate, Derbyshire: Amber Lane, 1981), p. 139-42.
'Green Room', *Plays and Players*, Oct. 1981, p. 49-50.
'Opportunities for Blasting Off', *New Statesman*,
 16 Oct. 1981. [Review of *A Better Class of Person*, by
 John Osborne.]
'Ah, Mischief: the Role of Public Broadcasting', *Ah! Mischief:
 the Writer and Television*, ed. Frank Pike (Faber, 1982),
 p. 41-50.
'I Still Have the Unfashionable Belief', *The Guardian*,
 3 Feb. 1983, p. 12.
'Dole for the Arts', *The Guardian*, 29 Mar. 1984, p. 12.
 [Review of *The Culture Club*, by Bryan Appleyard.]
'Nicaragua: an Appeal', *Granta*, No. 16, 1985, p. 232-6.
 [Speech of Jan. 1985 at 'A Night for Nicaragua' concert.]
'How to Spend a Million', *Sunday Times*, 3 Mar. 1985, p. 39.
 [On *Wetherby*.]
'Sailing Downwind with *Pravda*', *The Observer*, 9 Nov. 1986,
 p. 10.
'David Hare', *The Joint Stock Book*, ed. Rob Ritchie
 (Methuen, 1987), p. 105-10.
'Why I Shall Vote Labour', *The Spectator*, 23 May 1987,
 p. 14.
'Diary', *The Spectator*, 27 Feb., 5 Mar., 7, 14 May 1988.

Interviews

Ronald Hayman, 'David Hare', *The Times*, 22 May 1971.

Peter Ansorge, 'Explorations: Portable Playwrights', *Plays and Players*, Feb. 1972, p. 18, 20.

Hugh Hebert, 'Putting the Knuckle in', *The Guardian*, 4 Mar. 1974, p. 8.

Peter Ansorge, 'Current Concerns', *Plays and Players*, July 1974, p. 18-22.

Ronald Hayman, 'David Hare: Coming out of a Different Trap', *The Times*, 30 Aug. 1975.

Ann McFerran, 'End of the Acid Era', *Time Out*, 29 Aug. 1975, p. 12-15.

'From Portable Theatre to Joint Stock . . . via Shaftesbury Avenue', *New Theatre Voices of the Seventies*, ed. Simon Trussler (Methuen, 1981), p. 110-20 [reprinted from *Theatre Quarterly*, No. 20, Dec. 1975-Feb. 1976, p. 108-15].

Steve Grant, 'Peace and Plenty', *Time Out*, 7 Apr. 1978, p. 15.

Ray Conolly, 'Dreams of the Man in a Cricket Sweater', *Evening Standard*, 3 Aug. 1979, p. 25.

Michael Billington, 'Broken Rules', *Radio Times*, 12 Jan. 1980, p. 17.

Discussion, 'After *Fanshen*', *Performance and Politics in Popular Drama*, ed. David Bradby, Louis James, and Bernard Sharratt (Cambridge University Press, 1980), p. 297-314.

Judy Dempsey, 'Interview with David Hare', *Literary Review*, 22 Aug. 1980, p. 35-6.

Benedict Nightingale, 'An Angry Young Man of the Eighties Brings His Play to New York', *New York Times*, 17 Oct. 1982, Sec. II, p. 1, 6.

Joan Goodman, 'New World', *The Observer*, 23 Jan. 1983, p. 44.

Angela Wilkes, 'Making Fun of Fleet Street', *Sunday Times*, 16 Dec. 1984.

Michael Billington, 'What Excites Me about *Pravda*', *The Guardian*, 2 Mar. 1985, p. 12.

Jim Hiley, 'The Wetherby Report', *The Observer Magazine*, 10 Mar. 1985, p. 64-5.

Steve Grant, 'Act All about It', *The Observer*, 28 Apr. 1985, p. 21.

Francis Wheen, 'Newshounds', *Tatler*, May 1985, p. 22, 24.

Steve Lawson, 'Hare Apparent', *Film Comment*, Sept.-Oct. 1985,
    p. 18-22.
Mel Gussow, 'David Hare: Playwright as Provocateur', *New York
    Times Magazine*, 29 Sept. 1985, p. 42, 44-7, 75-6.
W. J. Wetherby, 'Plenty of Hare', *The Guardian*, 19 Oct. 1985, p. 11.
Dan Yakir, 'Hare Style', *Horizon*, Dec. 1985, p. 45-7.
Carol Homden, 'A Dramatist of Surprise', *Plays and Players*,
    Sept. 1988, p. 5-7.
Vera Lustig, 'Soul Searching', *Drama*, No. 4, 1988, p. 15, 17-18.
John Dugdale, 'Love, Death and Edwina', *The Listener*, 15 Sept. 1988,
    p. 38-9.
Robert Crew, 'Playwright Hare Feels the Sting of Controversy',
    Toronto Star, 11 Feb. 1989, Sec. F, p. 3.
Diane Selway, 'David Hare', *European Travel and Life* (New York),
    Oct. 1989, p. 79-80, 82, 86.

b: Secondary Sources

Jonathan Rice, 'All the School's a Stage', *Daily Telegraph Magazine*,
    9 Aug. 1974, p. 22-3, 25-6.
Peter Ansorge, *Disrupting the Spectacle* (Pitman, 1975), p. 10-13, 18-21.
John Peter, 'Meet the Wild Bunch', *Sunday Times*, 11 July 1976, p. 31.
Albert Hunt, 'Theatre of Violence', *New Society*, 4 Nov. 1976, p. 261-2.
Oleg Kerensky, *The New British Drama* (Hamish Hamilton, 1977),
    p. 175-87.
Peter Ansorge, 'David Hare: a War on Two Fronts', *Plays and Players*,
    Apr. 1978, p. 12-16.
Ronald Hayman, *British Theatre since 1955: a Reassessment*
    (Oxford University Press, 1979), p. 92-6, 113-18.
Steve Grant, 'Voicing the Protest: the New Writers', *Dreams and
    Deconstructions*, ed. Sandy Craig (Ambergate, Derbyshire:
    Amber Lane, 1980), p. 117-27.
Catherine Itzin, *Stages in the Revolution* (Eyre Methuen, 1980),
    p. 330-6.
C. W. E. Bigsby, 'The Language of Crisis in British Theatre',
    Contemporary English Drama, ed. C.W.E. Bigsby (Arnold, 1981),
    p. 11-51.
John Russell Taylor, 'In and Out of Court', *Plays and Players*,
    Jan. 1982, p. 12-14.
Roger N. Cornish, 'David Hare', *British Dramatists since World
    War II: Dictionary of Literary Biography, Vol. 13* (Detroit: Gale,
    1982), p. 234-42.

Gunther Klotz, *Britischer Dramatiker der Gegenwart* (Berlin: Henschelverlag, 1982), p. 237-58.

Jeremy Ridgman, ' "A Shameful Conquest of Itself": Images from the Empire in Post-War British Drama', *Australasian Drama Studies*, I, No. 1, Oct. 1982, p. 89-108.

Jonathan Myerson, 'David Hare: Fringe Graduate', *Drama*, Autumn 1983, p. 26-8.

John Bull, *New British Political Dramatists* (Macmillan, 1984), p. 60-94.

Tony Dunn, 'The Play of Politics', *Drama*, No. 2, 1985, p. 13-15.

William Harris, 'Mapping the World of David Hare', *American Theatre*, Dec. 1985, p. 12-17.

D. Keith Peacock, 'Chronicles of Wasted Time', *Historical Drama: Themes in Drama, Vol. 8* (Cambridge University Press, 1986), p. 195-212.

David Ian Rabey, *British and Irish Political Drama in the Twentieth Century* (Macmillan, 1986), p. 166-75.

Richard Allen Cave, *New British Drama in Performance on the London Stage, 1970 to 1985* (Gerrards Cross: Colin Smythe, 1987), p. 175-212.

Colin Chambers and Mike Prior, *Playwrights' Progress* (Oxford: Amber Lane, 1987), p. 179-88.

Michelene Wandor, *Look Back in Gender* (Methuen, 1987), p. 109-15.

Douglas Kennedy, 'Two Britains', *New Statesman and Society*, 14 Oct. 1988, p. 36-7.